**Anatomy
of the
Ship**

THE SHIPS OF CHRISTOPHER COLUMBUS

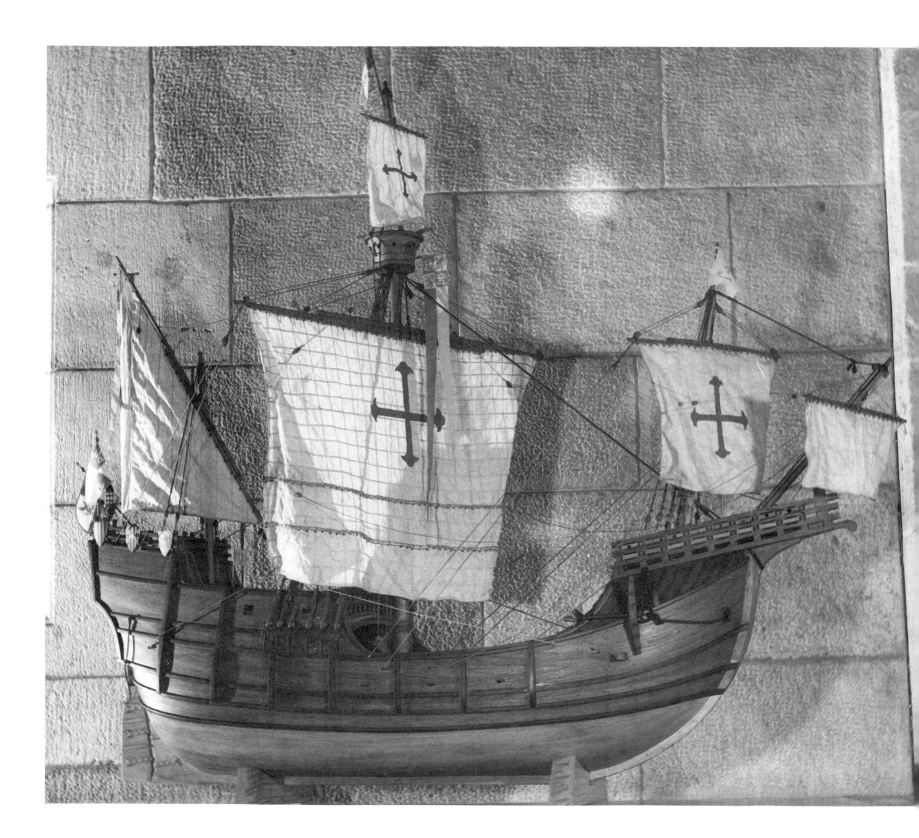

**Anatomy
of the
Ship**

THE SHIPS OF CHRISTOPHER COLUMBUS

SANTA MARIA ❖ NIÑA ❖ PINTA

Xavier Pastor

Naval
Institute
Press

Frontispiece
A model of the *Santa Maria* as a nao,
based on the research of Martinez-Hidalgo.
The 1991–2 replicas of all three of the
Columbus ships are based on his work.
Museu Maritim, Barcelona

© Xavier Pastor 1992

First published in Great Britain 1992 by
Conway Maritime Press Limited,
101 Fleet Street,
London EC4Y 1DE

Published and distributed in the United States
of America and Canada by the Naval Institute Press,
118 Maryland Avenue, Annapolis,
Maryland 21402–5035

Library of Congress Catalog Card No.
92–60240

ISBN 1–55750–755–4

Manufactured in Great Britain

Contents

ACKNOWLEDGEMENTS

I have expressed my gratitude to some of the most important contributors to the creation of this book in the Foreword, but there are other friends and institutions also without whom the project could not have been completed. Amongst these, I would like to thank:

The management and staff of the Museu Maritim at Barcelona, for help in searching out material from the archives, particularly photographs;

The Director of the Museo Naval at Madrid, who allowed me, some years ago, to take photographs at the museum, and also allowed the use of material from books and documents in the museum;

My friend Manuel Ripoll, who supplied an old photograph of Guillén's *Santa Maria* (his father, a doctor in the Navy, was the ship's doctor aboard the replica; and

Antonio Jaen, draughtsman, who was able to provide me with a copy of a lines plan which was no longer in print. His father had drawn the plans of the *Santa Maria* and the caravels for the Martinez-Hidalgo project.

Foreword

It will rapidly become clear to the reader that this book does not fit easily into the pattern set by the other titles in the Anatomy series. Each previous volume was written by a specialist possessing full knowledge of the vessel under examination. The authors were able to base their descriptions on archival material like plans or on contemporary drawings or photographs. Even in the case of *Susan Constant*, by Brian Lavery – the subject nearest in time to Columbus's *Santa Maria* – the author was able to support his statements in part by reference to construction standards of the period.

This is, unfortunately, far from being the case with the ships of Christopher Columbus. There is now no technical information available on how ships were built in Spain in the fifteenth century. The *Itinerario de Navegacion* by J Escalante de Mendoza (published in 1575 – 83 years after Columbus's voyage) contains only rules of a general character dealing with the materials used in shipbuilding, such as the timber most suitable for hull and masts or the appropriate vegetable fibres for manufacturing rigging and sails; the author gave no information at all on the dimensions of parts of the hull nor on the standing or running rigging.

Shipbuilding treatises in which technical standards are recorded do not appear in Spain until about a century after Columbus. The first was the *Instruccion Nautica para Navegar* by Diego Garcia del Palacio in 1587. In 1611, 24 years later, the *Arte para Fabricar, Fortificar y Aparejar Naos* by Thome Cano was published. This book represents an early attempt to trace the evolution of the concepts underlying the construction of galleons.

It is against this lack of hard contemporary information that any attempt to reconstruct the ships of Christopher Columbus has to be seen. If a large measure of agreement has generally been reached in the past century over the design and construction of the two smaller ships, the *Niña* and the *Pinta*, the same cannot be said of the *Santa Maria*. Interpretations of the design, construction and even basic ship type of Columbus's flagship have differed widely since 1892. It is therefore the case that an attempt to describe the *Santa Maria* only in terms of the current reconstruction, built in Spain to commemorate the 500th anniversary of the European discovery of America, is clearly inadequate. To set this reconstruction in its context, the replica built by Martinez-Hidalgo and the two official versions built in Spain on previous occasions have also to be examined.

Furthermore, a brief summary of the origin and development of the caravel is necessary. Not only were the other two ships of Columbus's fleet on his first voyage vessels of this type, but also the caravel as a type had played a key role in the Portuguese exploration of the African coasts in the years prior to Columbus's voyage. In this sense the development and use of the caravel can indeed be said to have made possible the European discovery of America.

The lack of reference material forced the designers of the earlier reconstructions of Columbus's ships to base the lines of the *Santa Maria* on engravings or drawings in nautical charts of the period. Only on the rigging were the three designers in agreement, for an entry in Columbus's logbook gives details which leave no room for doubt. The tonnage and length of the earlier reconstructions of the *Santa Maria* were also based on an entry in the logbook in which the ship's launch is mentioned, but the references were misinterpreted both by the French archaeologist Auguste Jal and later by Fernández-Duro, followed by Guillén.

The only three-dimensional testimony to fifteenth-century ships is an ex-voto dated 1450, whose history will be discussed below, as far as it is known. Its proportions – which could be exaggerated, as they do not show the generally accepted ratio between length and breadth – have not been used to determine the shape of the current reconstruction of the *Santa Maria* as a nao, but it was the source of important information on the system of shipbuilding in the Mediterranean at the time, and also on the peculiarities of particular parts of the structure of contemporary ships, which could not be deduced from graphic evidence of the period.

Guillén's thesis that the *Santa Maria* was a caravel has now been rejected by historians and archaeologists of all nations. Martinez-Hidalgo, in a section of his fully documented book *Las Naves de Colón* – today considered the best argued exposition of the category of ship to which the *Santa Maria* belonged – considers her to have been a nao. He bases his theory on the fact that Columbus made no fewer than eighty-one references to the ship as such in his logbook.

It is with pleasure that I record my thanks to José María Martinez-Hidalgo y Terán for the great help and encouragement which I have received from conversations with him, as well as for his permission to draw on the contents of his book, some passages of which have been incorporated into this work.

Another part of this book is based on a series of articles of mine which were published in the Spanish magazine *Yate y Motonautica* in 1977, and later translated into English by that excellent model builder and good friend the late Sydney J Mostyn of Blackpool, England.

The revision of the present work, written in my poor English, was undertaken by my old friend Robert James Kenyon.

Perhaps the most important contribution to the creation of this book was that of my wife Nuria. She had patience enough to put up with my many hours of concentration both at the drawing table and in front of the word processor, the only member of the team to offer less than total support.

Xavier Pastor   **Mallorca, October 1991**

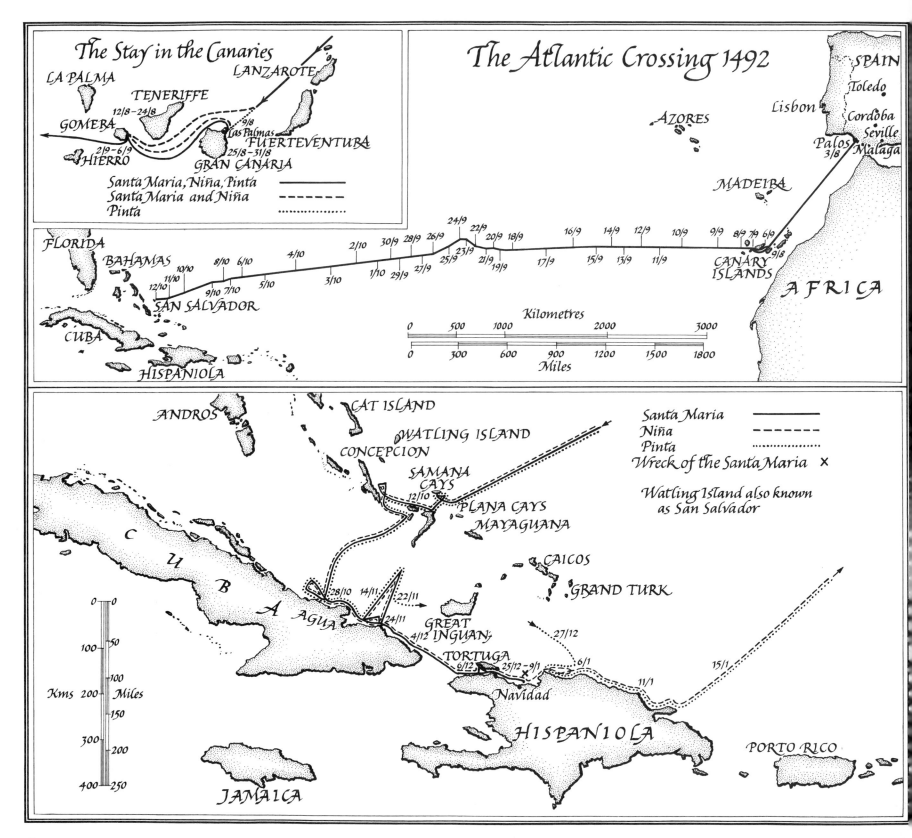

The Stay in the Canaries

LA PALMA
LANZAROTE
TENERIFFE
12/8–24/8
9/8
GOMERA
Las Palmas
FUERTEVENTURA
2/9–6/9
25/8–31/8
HIERRO
GRAN CANARIA

Santa Maria, Niña, Pinta ——————
Santa Maria and Niña – – – – – –
Pinta ·····················

The Atlantic Crossing 1492

SPAIN
Toledo
Lisbon
Córdoba
Seville
AZORES
Palos
3/8
Málaga

MADEIRA

FLORIDA
BAHAMAS
24/9
22/9
20/9
18/9
16/9
14/9
12/9
10/9
9/9
8/9 7/9 6/9
25/9 23/9
21/9
19/9
17/9
15/9
13/9
11/9
9/8
CANARY
ISLANDS
2/10
30/9 28/9 26/9
10/10
8/10 6/10
4/10
12/10
9/10 7/10
5/10
3/10
1/10 29/9 27/9
AFRICA
SAN SALVADOR

CUBA

HISPANIOLA

Kilometres
0   500   1000   2000   3000
0   300   600   900   1200   1500   1800
Miles

ANDROS
CAT ISLAND
WATLING ISLAND
CONCEPCION
SAMANA
CAYS
12/10
PLANA CAYS
MAYAGUANA

Santa Maria ——————
Niña – – – – – –
Pinta ·····················
Wreck of the Santa Maria ✕

Watling Island also known
as San Salvador

C
U
B
A
28/10 14/11
22/11
AGUA
24/11
GREAT
INGUAN
4/12
TORTUGA
6/12
25/12–9/1
✕
Navidad

CAICOS
GRAND TURK

27/12

6/1
11/1
15/1

0   0
100   50
100
200   150
Kms 200 Miles
300   200
400   250

JAMAICA

HISPANIOLA

PORTO RICO

Introduction

THE VOYAGE

The ships of Columbus's small fleet sailed from the port of Palos, Huelva, southern Spain, on 2 August 1492, following the ebb tide along the river Odiel to the Saltes sand bar. They set sail for the ocean passage at 0800hrs the following day, at a speed of 4 knots, heading for the Canary Islands. The passage to the Canaries took six days, in the course of which the *Pinta* required a jury repair to her rudder. The nearest port to Spain was Lanzarote, which at the time belonged to the Spanish Crown, while the rest of the Islands were still in the possession of the Guanche people.

The *Pinta*, commanded by Martin Alonso Pinzón, remained off Gran Canaria while the commanders sought a substitute vessel or a means of repairing her rudder permanently. On 11 August the *Santa Maria* and *Niña* headed for Gomera Island, while the *Pinta* was repaired at Gando, Gran Canaria. Columbus meanwhile set about converting the lateen rigged *Niña* for square sails on the foremast and mainmast. The *Santa Maria* and *Niña* returned to Las Palmas, arriving on 25 August.

On 1 September 1492 the flotilla sailed from Las Palmas de Gran Canaria, heading for Gomera, about 90 sea miles away. They departed Gomera at sunrise on 6 September, after having heard Mass and taken provisions on board.

By 12 September the ships had run 2400 miles, and Columbus believed they were now in the waters of Cipango, today known as Japan.

They reached the Sargasso Sea on the 16th; Columbus was the first European navigator to cross this region of the Atlantic Ocean. During the crossing Columbus took account, for the first time, of magnetic deviation; by 30 September the needle had deviated 11¼ degrees west.

As days passed with the ships making little headway into the adverse trade winds, the fears of the crews over the length of the voyage and the unknown dangers awaiting them increased steadily. By Sunday 7 October the flotilla was at latitude 28 degrees, 2 degrees south of Gomera, and at about longitude 67 degrees west. The course was changed from west to WSW, and after a four-day run the flotilla had reached latitude 24 degrees in the region of the trade winds.

On Saturday 20 September, crew members saw a kind of sea bird which rarely flies more than 30 leagues from the coast. On 1 October four birds flew across together, and on the 3rd a flock of more than forty birds was seen. Columbus began to fear that he had sailed between the islands, leaving Cipango astern.

In the ships there were whisperings and protests. Some chroniclers report that the sailors voiced a wish not to go further.

On 11 October, after some days sailing in pleasant conditions, the crews began almost continuously to spot birds and vegetation floating out from the shore. They picked up a reed and a carved pole. Columbus, on the aftercastle, saw a light in the darkness: 'It was like a little candle which rose and fell', he noted in his logbook. It was the first sight of the New World.

Some historians maintain that this episode was an invention, recorded in the logbook with the aim of winning the reward of 10,000 *maravedies* (about £250 sterling today) for the first crew member to see the coast. Nevertheless, tests made on the rocky coast of High Cay in the Bahamas by Ruth G Wolper Durlacher in 1959 and confirmed by later experiments such as those of Dr Paolo Emilio Taviani in 1975, proved that a bonfire lit there can indeed be seen from the sea at a distance of 46 kilometres (29 miles), approximately the position of the *Santa Maria* on 11 October.

At 0200hrs on 12 October Juan Rodriguez Bermejo, also known as Rodrigo de Triana, sighted land. It was the rocky coast of High Cay, southeast of San Salvador, which its inhabitants called Guanahani. Historians have since identified Guanahani as Watling Island in the Bahama group.

On 14 October Columbus launched a boat with an armed landing party and headed for the coast. Accompanied by the Pinzón brothers, the captains of the two caravels, he landed on the beach carrying the expedition's green cross flag and took possession of the land in the name of the King and Queen of Spain. The act was formally recorded by the fleet notary Rodrigo de Escobedo in the presence of a crowd of naked natives. The encounter of two worlds had occurred. Columbus sailed along the coast of the island and paid a visit to the nearby villages.

Later the same day the flotilla set sail on a southwesterly course. They visited Concepcion (Rum Cay), Fernandina (Long Island) and Isabela (Crooked Island). On 28 October they arrived off Cuba and dropped anchor near the modern Porto Samá, on the northeastern coast. After two weeks exploring southeastwards along the coast, they attempted on 14 November to make the passage back to Isabela, but were forced by squalls to turn back towards the Cuban coast.

On the 22nd Martin Alonso Pinzón in the *Pinta* became separated from the other vessels, and made his way eastwards towards Great Inagua. The *Santa Maria* and *Niña* set course first westward because of the current, then southeastward along the Cuban coast towards Cayo Grande de Moa. Columbus, obsessed by the idea that he was in the country of Cipango, was hoping to find the lands which Marco Polo had discovered and the Great Khan's court.

In early December 1492 the *Niña* and the *Santa Maria* crossed the Windward Passage to Hispaniola. The local Indians informed Columbus that there was gold in Tortuga (later famous as a pirate stronghold) and Cibao island. Columbus thought he had found the land of his dreams.

On 24 December, with the ships in calm waters near Cap Haïtien and the crews resting, the helm of the *Santa Maria* was taken by an unskilled ship's boy. The ship struck coral reefs and the hull was split open between the frames.

Columbus built a fort named Navidad from the wreckage of the ship, with a garrison of thirty-nine and guns, supplies and articles to barter for gold with the natives. He himself boarded the *Niña* to continue the exploration.

After a rendezvous with the *Pinta* off the north coast of Hispaniola, Columbus explored eastwards along the coast as far as Cabo Samana, and the two ships began the return voyage to Spain in mid January 1493.

On his second voyage, Columbus arrived at the site of the Navidad Fort in November 1493, to find that the garrison had been slaughtered only twenty days earlier and the fort burnt and completely destroyed.

THE FERNANDEZ-DURO REPLICA (1892): THE SANTA MARIA AS A NAO

The first replica of the *Santa Maria* was built to commemorate the 400th anniversary of the European discovery of America. The ship was built in Cadiz, and based on research undertaken by a Commission presided over by Captain Cesáreo Fernández-Duro. Her destination was the Columbus World Fair at Chicago, as a gift from the government and people of Spain. She sailed across the Atlantic under the command of Captain Victor M Concas.

This replica was built as a nao. Her proportions were extrapolated from the conjectural length of the longboat of the prototype *Santa Maria* (a measurement itself subsequently proving to be based on a mistaken interpretation of an entry in Columbus's logbook). Though the ornamental details on the replica were unusual for a late fifteenth century vessel – this was a period in which ship decoration was austere – the general conception of the replica as a nao found widespread support among historians at the time.

Hull

The hull was short, wide and very high, full and flat of bottom, with few runs. The stem and sternpost sections were very robust in order to support the structures at the stern and bow. The frames, at their upper ends, inclined inboard to give pronounced tumblehome, making the deck somewhat closed. The hull was reinforced with three longitudinal strakes, with thirteen vertical futtock riders (*bulárcamas*) on each side of the ship like exterior frames, twelve of them uniformly separated. The lower ends of these riders were half a metre above the waterline and morticed into the lowest strake; they diverged slightly as they rose up to the gunwale. The thirteenth rider (the aftermost) was shorter, and began one metre above the waterline, with its upper end at the level of the poop deck.

The stern transom bore an escutcheon, which was one of the most criticised features of the project, since this type of stern decoration did not appear until the beginning of sixteenth century. It incorporated a tiller port (*limera*) through which the tiller entered the hull. The broad bladed rudder narrowed in cut steps to the head. On each side of the tiller port were hawse holes.

The ship had one main deck with two open hatchways; the quarterdeck was also fitted with a hatchway. Over the quarterdeck was the poop. The forecastle was triangular in shape, with gunwales almost a metre in height;

Table 1: **SANTA MARIA AS A NAO (FERNANDEZ-DURO, 1982)**

Keel length	18.5m	60ft	8½in
Waterline length	21.7m	71ft	5in
Length between perpendiculars	22.6m	74ft	1in
Maximum length	39.1m	128ft	3½in
Width	7.8m	25ft	8½in
Depth of hold	3.8m	12ft	6in
Draught amidships	2.6m	8ft	6in
Draught forward	2.2m	7ft	2½in
Draught aft	3.0m	10ft	
Displacement	233.0 tons		

its forward extremity overhung the stem by almost half the forecastle's total length. It was fitted with hawse holes on both sides for the anchor warps.

Rigging

The reconstruction was rigged with three masts, a bowsprit and a poop boomkin. The foremast had a slight inclination towards the prow, and was crossed by a yard consisting of two pieces. The yard was raised by a double halliard and tackle and had lifts and braces on the yardarms. The foresail carried bowlines, clewlines, and buntlines for hauling up the foot of the sail. On each lower clew three blocks were attached for the clewlines, sheets and tacks. It is possible that sheets and tacks were single ropes. There were no channels for this mast.

The mainmast was perpendicular to the waterline, reinforced with wooldings and supported laterally by eight shrouds turned in and linked to the channels with deadeyes and lanyards. This system was taken from a high relief work which can be seen in the church of San Nicolas in Burgos, carved between 1480 and 1503. The shrouds were fitted with ratlines. The mainmast carried a circular top whose base rested on trestletrees.

The mainyard was also of two pieces whipped together with lashings, and crossed the mainmast about two metres below the top. The rigging was similar to that of the foresail but proportionately larger. The mainsail area could be increased by the addition of one or two bonnets.

Above the top, the mainmast was crossed by a single yard, on which the topsail was set. The foot of this sail had a large roach to prevent chafing on the rim of the top.

The mizzen mast was somewhat shorter in length than the foremast and was sited on the quarterdeck, with a slight rake towards the poop. Its two-piece lateen yard was held to the mast by a simplified parrel. (In Spain, the lower part of the yard is called *car* and the upper *pena*). The sail was a lateen and its area was half that of the mainsail without bonnets. The tack led aft to a boomkin run out aft from the poop deck.

The bowsprit was one fifth shorter in length than the mizzen mast and was fastened to the stem with a bobstay and gammoned to the cutwater, angled upwards at 40 degrees to the horizontal. The spritsail yard ran along the bowsprit on an iron traveller, similar to that employed in regional craft such as the *laud* and the *falucho* even today. Details of this rig can be seen in the drawings included below.

On 30 July 1892, Fernández-Duro's reconstruction of the *Santa Maria* was towed from La Carraca dockyard to the port of Cadiz by the steamer *egazpi*, and was saluted there by Spanish and foreign ships. The following day she was towed as far as Huelva by the *Pielago*, and then navigated under sail to Palos de Moguer, at the mouth of the river Odiel. She put to sea from here on 3 August in a symbolic departure, on the same day that Columbus had set sail 400 years earlier. She was then towed to the open sea by the cruiser *Isla de Luzon*, escorted by two lines of ships from different nations. When a light breeze blew, the *Santa Maria* set sail and, at the head of the naval procession, proceeded between two lines of warships from many different countries of the world. The English ships present at this symbolic send-off were HMS *Australia*, HMS *Amphion*, HMS *Scout* and two torpedo boats whose names I have been unable to trace. The farewell ceremony was short, because the ships had to cross the Saltes bar to enter the port before low tide.

From Palos, the *Santa Maria* was towed to La Carraca dockyard, near Cadiz, on 26 August. She remained there while additional work was carried out to increase the accommodation for her crew, which was rather larger than originally intended; the ballast was also moved to improve the seaworthiness of the ship. Supplies and food were embarked and stowed wherever there was room, because stowage details had not been considered fully by the archaeological commission in charge of the design. All this took considerable time.

On 10 February 1893 the *Santa Maria* set sail for Las Palmas in the Canary Islands. From there, she left for Santa Cruz de Tenerife. On the evening of 22 February she set sail from Santa Cruz to San Juan de Puerto Rico, where she arrived on 30 March, after thirty six days of sailing, one fewer than Columbus's voyage. Before her arrival in Chicago on 7 July 1893, the *Santa Maria* called at Havana, New York, Quebec, Montreal, Charlotte (on Lake Ontario) and Toronto.

THE GUILLÉN REPLICA (1927): THE SANTA MARIA AS A CARAVEL

In 1927 Julio F Guillén y Tato, then a Lieutenant in the Spanish Navy, produced a documented study for a new reconstruction of the historic vessel, published as the book *La Carabela Santa Maria*. It was the starting point for the construction of a replica which featured in the Exposicion Iberoamericana in Seville. When I was able to obtain a copy of the book in 1940, it was already rare owing to the small number of copies originally published. The book not only detailed the first-hand research of the author in libraries and archives, but also contained an extensive repertoire of notes on the observations of previous authors on the Columbus ships, and Guillén's reasons for concluding that the *Santa Maria* had been a carabela de armada, not a nao.

The book contains numerous drawings in a clear and distinctive style; for the non-expert these constitute a valuable source of additional information on the construction, masting, rigging, ordnance, equipment, flags, shields and conditions of life aboard, all essential to a knowledge of the period.

Guillén was for many years Director of the Museo Naval in Madrid, a member of the Academia de la Historia and a prolific writer. Other historians such as Gervasio de Artiñano and Pelayo Alcala Galiano had already drawn attention to the anachronistic decoration of the Fernández-Duro replica. In England, W S Laird Clowes voiced similar concern in commenting on a model of the replica which the Spanish Government presented to the Science Museum in London. Henrique Quirino da Fonseca in Portugal

and Enrico D'Albertis in Italy were equally doubtful of the absolute authenticity of the earlier replica.

Contrary to the opinion of most historians and marine archaeologists, however, Guillén considered the *Santa Maria* to have been a caravel. He based his belief on traditional interpretations and upon two quotations from Columbus's logbook. The new reconstruction of the *Santa Maria* as a caravel was undertaken in the Echevarrieta shipyard in Cadiz, southern Spain.

Hull

The hull dimensions were derived, amongst other sources, from the accepted rules for measurements of caravels of 150 to 180 tons contained in a document included in the *Livro Nautico*, a manuscript from the Biblioteca Nacional of Lisbon, which refers to caravels with four masts, two square sails and two lateens. The documents included are dated about a century after Columbus's voyage.

The formulaic length for this replica was taken as the length on deck. The depth of hold was measured from the upper edge of the keel up to the lower face of the main beam.

The frames were fixed to the keel with a keelson, and according to the *Livro Nautico* a caravel of this size carried twenty-four frames with spaces of some 80cm (2.62ft). The floor timbers extended some 2.5 metres (8.2ft) to each side of the keel.

The prow was very full, as is frequently shown in drawings of caravels, and there was no forecastle. Protection for crew members engaged in fighting, and shelter from waves, was provided in the form of a small, very low deck with gunwales called the *tilla*.

The tuck of the stern had very pronounced curves in order to support the weight of the structure above. The transom, supporting the poop and mounted on the head of the sternpost, had a length of rather over half the breadth of the ship. In the upper part of the transom was the tiller port, through which the tiller passed into the hull at main deck level to the compass room, from which the ship was steered.

The binnacle was installed in a type of cabinet fitted with a wooden bowl which contained the card (marked with thirty-two bearings even in the fifteenth century). The compass needle was a magnetised iron bar which had periodically to be gently stroked with a loadstone to conserve its properties. The compass was covered with glass and the cabinet had a specially designed lamp, whose faint light made the compass visible at night.

The rudder was constructed of vertical planks fastened together by iron bands, and it was held to the sternpost by pintles and gudgeons.

The quarterdeck was approximately 1.6 metres (5ft 2½in) above the main deck and its foremost beam was only slightly aft of the after face of the mainmast. Over the quarterdeck was Columbus's simple cabin.

Table 2: SANTA MARIA AS A CARAVEL (GUILLEN, 1927)

Length	25.6m	84ft	
Keel length	18.6m	61ft	
Rake of stem	6.1m	20ft	1in
Rake of stern	1.1m	3ft	6in
Extreme width	7.5m	24ft	8½in
Main beam sheer	0.9m	2ft	11in
Floor timber	2.5m	8ft	2½in
Displacement	185.0 tons		

The aft structure of the upperworks was known also as the stern castle. Its deck was limited by stanchions topped with a rail.

The hull featured a very strong wale at the level of the waterline. Two further wales, beneath the main wale, were separated by some 50cm (about 1ft 8in) at the level of the main frame, and converged towards the stem and stern. The fenders or riders, further reinforcing the hull, numbered eleven and ran from the upper edge of the second wale to the gunwale, raked forward or aft according to their positions. The three aftmost riders ran from the upper edge of the main wale; the foremost of the three rose as far as the upper rail of the stern castle, while the other two rose to the level of the stern castle deck.

The outer sides of the stern castle were vertical without any decoration other than the exterior buttock riders, wales and sheer rails, which bordered spaces proportional in form and dimension.

Masting and rigging

The Guillén replica was masted as had been the Fernández-Duro version. The rigging, too, was in essence similar to that of the earlier replica. Guillén sought to avoid controversy by following essentially Columbus's own logbook entry regarding the sails carried:

> . . . it was with little wind until midday, when it changed to blow more amicably and the nao carried all sails, main and two bonnets, and foresail, and spritsail, and mizzen, and topsail, and the bark on the poop. [24 October 1492]

Only minor changes, for instance in the shape and rigging of the topsail, were made.

The theoretical basis for the masting, sails and running rigging was left somewhat sketchy, since some characteristics of the rig survived in practical use until the first half of the twentieth century in Mediterranean fishing and working craft. Among the sources which were, however, used by Guillén, the *Arte para Fabricar, Fortificar y Aparejar Naos* by Thome Cano (published in Seville in 1611) is notable. The proportions given by Cano were appropriate for ships built a century or so after Columbus, and Guillén's theoretical mainmast length – 2½ times the beam – is taken from this source. The main yard was given a theoretical length of 2⅓ times the beam, a standard taken from *Instruccion Nautica para Navegar* (published in Mexico in 1587). Nevertheless, when the replica was constructed the mainmast was made markedly longer than the proportional length specified by Cano.

The standing rigging of the *Santa Maria* as a caravel consisted of six pairs of shrouds fixed to the mast above the floor of the top, through which they passed through holes. There were also two backstays at the pole head. All shrouds and backstays were tightened with deadeyes and landyards set in long channels fixed to the hull and secured to it with chainplates. The ratlines were fitted only between the two or three foremost shrouds.

The mizzen and foremast were each fitted with two pairs of shrouds, of lesser diameter and secured at the waterways of the quarterdeck and *tilla* respectively. They also had pendants with burton tackles.

There were two forestays, one secured on the forward third of the bowsprit and the other near the bowsprit cap.

The topsail was set on a small yard above the top. It was gored at a wide angle because the clews were reeved through blocks on the mainyard, belaying at the topsail bitt at the foot of the mast. The topsail also had a large roach to clear the rim of the top.

The mizzen sail, also called a water sail, was set on a typical lateen yard.

This yard consisted of two spars lashed and whipped together, and wa hoisted by a simple halliard, reeving through a single block fastened to th head of the mast or through a sheave worked there. The tacks were fitted t the lower arm of the yard, and the crowsfeet for the topping lift to the uppe third. The yard was held to the mast by a single parrel, similar to that use in coastal fishing craft in the Mediterranean until recently. The yard wa fitted with one vang on each side of the sail, rigged on the upper third of th yard. The mizzen sheet, leading from the clew, rove through a sheave at th end of a boomkin extended from the poop and was belayed at the heel o the boomkin.

After being exhibited at the Exposicion Iberoamericana de Sevilla (1927-9), this version of the *Santa Maria* was anchored off the monastery of L Rabida, at Huelva, southern Spain. In 1945 she sank off Alicante whil under tow from Valencia on the east coast to Cartagena for repairs.

THE REHABILITATION OF THE NAO: THE MARTINEZ HIDALGO PROJECT (1964)

José María Martinez-Hidalgo y Terán, a Commander in the Spanish Navy was the Director of the Museu Maritim at Barcelona for 28 years. H devoted 10 years of work to the production of new plans and models of th ships of Christopher Columbus. The full-size replica of the *Santa Mari* exhibited at the New York World Fair of 1964–5 was based on his work.

Howard I Chapelle, appointed by the Smithsonian Institution as an ad visor during the construction of the replica and also translator into Englis of Martinez-Hidalgo's book *Las Naves de Colón*, noted in his foreword 'I am convinced that the new presentations are advances on previous effort in all respects'.

Martinez-Hidalgo was convinced that the original interpretation of th *Santa Maria* as a nao had been correct, and his theories were supported b international maritime experts such as R C Anderson, Björn Landströn and Heinrich Winter. The promoter of the idea of a new reconstruction wa Lawrence Wineberg.

Construction of the new replica was undertaken by Astilleros Cardon but the finished vessel did not make her own passage across the Atlanti She was embarked on the German freighter *Neidenfeld* at Barcelona befor a crowd of curious onlookers, destination New York.

The replica was landed at Mench's Boulevard, Flushing. Though sh weighed 80 tons and was nearly 30 metres in length, she travelled the thre miles to the Fair grounds upon a transporter. The *New York Times* de scribed this journey as 'complicated and with more incidents than the re vessel experienced in the Sargasso Sea'. According to the inhabitants of th Queen's District of New York, through which she passed, the passage c the replica was the most important thing that had ever happened there. was necessary to cut tree branches and dismantle telephone cables an electric wiring along the route, and permission was required from fourtee separate authorities. No fewer than ninety-nine technicians oversaw th entire route, and the ship was escorted by a flotilla of police cars. After further stage of two miles she arrived at the Meadow Lake, in the heart c the Fair, where she remained, berthed and on display to the public.

Now, 26 years later, the most extensive research has only served to confirm the validity of Martinez-Hidalgo's conclusions about the Colum bus ships. It is widely accepted that his reconstructions provide the closes possible approximation of the characteristics of the ships which played th ead in the European discovery of America. The new replicas of all three vessels completed for the 500th anniversary celebrations of Columbus's voyage are based closely upon his work.

THE COLUMBUS SHIPS TODAY: THE 500TH ANNIVERSARY PROJECT (1991–2)

The construction of three replicas to commemorate the 500th anniversary of Columbus's voyage has been organised in Spain by the Instituto de Historia y Cultura Naval de España. The nao *Santa Maria* has been built by Astilleros Viudes in Barcelona, the caravel *Pinta* by Astilleros Reunidos of Isla Cristina, Huelva, and the caravel *Niña* at the Cartagena Dockyard.

In October 1992 all three vessels will cross the Atlantic, retracing the course of Columbus and his flotilla 500 years before.

The nao

The word 'nao' appears for the first time in the *Chronicle* of Alfonso XI of Castille, in 1343. Meaning simply 'ship', the term was used very generally at first. It implied a vessel with one or two masts and driven by square sails, such as those shown in *Las Cantigas* of Alfonso X. By Columbus's time the nao was a merchant ship, only later used for war. The proportions of the nao, already considered classical by the sixteenth century, were expressed by the formula 1:2:3 for the breadth, keel length and overall length as in Garcia del Palacio's nao of 400 tons, or for depth, breadth and overall length according to Thome Cano and Escalante de Mendoza, although the last of these authors actually recommended a depth equal to 0.45 of the breadth for naos.

This formula was not applied uniformly, which caused the proportions of naos to vary, nor always applied at all. Moreover, the burthen was not clearly defined since the units of measurement varied from region to region.

At first, naos in the Mediterranean carried only a lateen sail (so called by Northern seamen, although this kind of sail actually originated on the Arabian coasts). Towards the middle of the fourteenth century the lateen sail was replaced by a square sail on large vessels, and remained only on small coastal and fishing craft. The single mast and sail of the lateen rig became two masts: a main carrying a single square sail, and a mizzen mast carrying a lateen sail. The two large steering oars which were used in the Mediterranean until about the end of the thirteenth century had already been replaced by a single rudder attached to the sternpost. Further evolution of the rigging resulted in the appearance of a foremast on the forecastle, also carrying a square sail. The three masted ship was born.

Sources

In the reconstruction of the *Santa Maria* as a nao of the late fifteenth century, engravings and other graphic evidence were most important for determining the common characteristics of the type; preference was naturally given to material originating in Spain. The basic shape of the stem and keel, the rake of the sternpost, the rebates and the sheer and camber of the main deck in the Mataró nao (see below) were particularly important. The buttocks and run of the hull were taken from the superb representation of two naos in the altarpiece painted by Joan de Reixach (circa 1500) in the Museu d'Art de Catalunya, and also in an engraving in the *Peregrinationem in Terram Sanctam* by Bernard von Breydenbach (circa 1495), which shows the hull of a nao being caulked. The nao from the Benicasa chart (1482) in the Biblioteca dell'Università, Bologna, and those represented in Carpac-

cio's paintings were also considered. The 1502 edition of the *Llibre del Consolat y dels Fets maritims*, published in Barcelona, was the source of information for details such as the horizontal bit for the anchor cable under the forecastle deck, the poop and details of the masting and sails (for example wooldings and the horizontal seams of the sails). Martinez-Hidalgo avoided over-reliance on ships drawn on contemporary charts. Those in the drawings of Hispaniola Island in the library of Seville cathedral were attributed to Fernando Colón (Columbus's son), who was not on the first voyage; the chart was drawn in about 1530 and the sails of the larger of the ships do not correspond with Columbus's own description of the *Santa Maria*'s sails.

The Mataró nao is a particularly important source. It is surprising that such a model, possibly votive, on view for some centuries at the Ermita de San Simon in the Catalan coastal town of that name, was ignored by the authors of the first two reconstructions of the *Santa Maria*, Fernández-Duro and Guillén.

It is an important ex-voto which has been established as dating from the middle of the fifteenth century, and it must have been unknown to, or felt not to merit the attention of, both authors. Fernández-Duro may indeed have been unaware of the model, which may have disappeared from Spain in the course of the nineteenth century. Guillén, however, had no such excuse: the model appeared in the antique market abroad, first in Munich then in London and New York, round about 1920, and caused much commotion amongst experts there. It would seem logical that similar interest should have been aroused in Spain, the model's place of origin, at the same time. Later Henry B Culver and Morton Nance published the results of a thorough study of the model in an article entitled 'A Contemporary 15th Century Ship Model' which appeared in *The Mariner's Mirror*. In Holland, I W van Nouhuys, famous for his reconstruction of the *Halve Maen*, Henry Hudson's ship, wrote *The Model of a Spanish Caravel of the Beginning of the XVth Century*. Heinrich Winter published his well documented *Die Katalanische Nao von 1450* in 1956. The model itself was finally put on exhibition at Rotterdam.

The chief importance of this model is that it is the only extant contemporary representation of a medieval vessel. Its builder had good knowledge of ships' architecture, and was probably a shipwright. The studies carried out on the model have added greatly to the scant information available hitherto on the beams which protruded through the hull planking, the horizontal bit below the forecastle deck, the structure of the great arch which opens into this space, and a number of other features.

I had gained a good theoretical knowledge of the model through many years of collecting all available information about it. I found myself involved in the project of building a replica of the ex-voto, sponsored by the Barcelona Camara de Comercio, Industria y Navegacion, having been proposed by José Martinez-Hidalgo.

The then Director of the Museu Maritim of Barcelona, Dr Laureano Carbonell, Martinez-Hidalgo and I travelled to Rotterdam, and thanks to the kindness of Leo C Akveld, Curator of the Maritiem Museum Prins Hendrik, we were able to inspect carefully the Mataró nao and gain a better understanding of its construction details, the conservation of the wood and the state of the materials used in its construction. Mr Hardonk, who had drawn a set of very accurate plans of the model, was also with us, and it was a very profitable work session. It was possible for us to see the interior of the hull by means of a videotape made using an endoscope.

13

After returning home I spent a year making the replica. The finished model was shown in an exhibition held in La Lonja de Barcelona, at the beginning of 1985, to commemorate the First Centenary of the Camara de Comercio, and in July it was offered to the Museu Maritim, where it is now on permanent exhibition.

Hull

Although the authors of previous studies had deduced the dimensions of the *Santa Maria* from the theoretical length of the ship's boat, and another author, D'Albertis, had based her dimensions upon an assumed crew of forty men, Martinez-Hidalgo decided to establish the dimensions of his replica purely through her tonnage, based on a recorded burthen of over 100 tons. At the end of the fifteenth century, the ton was roughly equivalent to two barrels of wine. There were several kinds of barrel (*tonel*) in Spain, those used in Seville in the South differing from those used in Vizcaya in the North. The ton of Seville was chosen.

The figure of 100 tons for the *Santa Maria* was established by Columbus's contemporary Bartolomé de Las Casas, in his summary of the first voyage; Fernando Colón gave a burthen of 110 tons for the same nao and added that she drew three Genoese fathoms, something like 5ft 8½in. Escalante de Mendoza wrote in 1585 that Columbus's ships were small, just a little over 100 tons.

The procedure for determining the hull dimensions followed by Martinez-Hidalgo was, as he says in his book *Las Naves de Colón*, trial and error. Dimensions of beam, keel and length in the ratio of 1:2:3, with a depth in hold in proportion to the beam, were used to calculate the capacity and shape which would produce 100 tons burthen. Starting from these data, a half model was constructed in the workshops of the Museu Maritim, using the most probable lines of naos previous to 1492.

This half model was the basis for the study of the hull. Its sections were modified as the conception of the ship's lines changed and developed, but care was always taken to maintain the correct dimensions. From this study, working drawings were produced and corrections were made as necessary to both half model and drawings. Following the report of the author, when all alterations and adjustments had been made, a new calculation showed the capacity to be 106 tons. This was considered acceptable, and the rig was designed. The estimated weight of structure, spars, rigging and sails, ordnance and furnished stores were established and the draft verified, with stability calculations also being made. Then the definitive plans were drawn and two models were built. One of these was presented to the Smithsonian Institution.

That the *Santa Maria* had the nao's characteristic forecastle can be deduced from Columbus's logbook entry for October 11: 'At ten o'clock at night, standing at the stern castle, he saw a light . . . [and] begged and warned to them to keep a good watch at the forecastle'.

The full lines and strongly curved timbers of the *Santa Maria* required substantial longitudinals, such as bilge stringers, clamps and wales, as well as vertical futtock riders (*bulárcamas*), to support to the vessel fully when she was careened for repairs.

The transom stern of the replica, half the beam in width, is typical of Spanish naos. It rests on a cross beam slightly V-shaped, like that shown in the Mataró model, with the planking coming up round and full.

The hull has three wales, running from stern to stempost. Above the main rail forward is the raised forecastle, triangular in shape with handrails.

The area below the forecastle is the only place where the hull is clinker planked; this feature is apparent in the Mataró model and in illustration such as the nao shown in the Benicasa chart of 1492.

The frames are single futtocks, joined end to end at the centreline of th keel, and reinforced with double floor timbers across the keel and a keelso above. The space between frames is about 60cm (1ft 8in). This is the sam arrangement as in the Mataró model. At the stern, cant timbers and tran som timbers are used, while at the stem there are cant timbers and ster aprons. The deck beams rest on pillars stepped on the keelson. Thos which support the beams of the coamings are cut with steps for use a ladders. The inside of the hull is not planked, but the spaces betwee frames at the floor are filled with mortar.

The beams are arranged to give the main deck a marked sheer, and thei ends are secured to waterways, shelves and clamps. The beam ends whic can be seen projecting through the planking in the Mataró nao are no reproduced; these ceased to pierce the planking at least from the earl sixteenth century.

The wales are about 10cm, (3¾in) in width, and are rounded on th outside face; the remaining hull planking is 8cm (3³⁄₂₀in) wide. The hull i carvel planked, with seams caulked with oakum and tar.

The fastenings used in the reconstruction are wooden dowels an wrought iron nails.

The midsection of the hull coincides with the greatest beam at the level o the main deck, and there is no tumblehome at this point. There is a smal amount at the raised quarterdeck and at the sides of the poop cabin. Th stern is of round tuck style, its planking finishing on the sternpost, to whicl the rudder is attached by five sets of pintles and gudgeons. The rudder i fitted with a ringbolt to take the preventers. The tiller enters the hull to th main deck through a tiller port. The tiller was worked by a helmsma according to the pilot's orders, since he could not see the sails when steer ing. The tiller was worked either by hand or by steering tackles.

As noted above, the main deck has a sheer of about 3 feet. It has tw hatches, one large (about 4sq m in area). Between the mainmast an mizzen mast is a smaller hatch, under the quarterdeck, giving access to th hold. The coamings of both hatches are low and can be closed with plank covered by canvas to keep out the weather. A companionway hatch is set i the quarterdeck forward of the mizzen mast, fitted with a ladder.

The bulwarks of the forecastle, poop deck and the break of the quarter deck are made up from stanchions with a capping rail. In places (as show in the drawings) the space between the stanchions is filled by removabl washboards, called *falcas* in Catalonia, which are fitted into grooves worke in the sides of the stanchions; this feature is taken from the Mataró nao.

Hawse holes are made in the poop at the sides of the sternpost and in th bow, under the forecastle. In Columbus's time these were lead sheated an covered from the inside by wooden lids to prevent water being shipped i high seas. Sheaves for the foresail sheets are worked into the fashion tim bers at the waist, for the mainsail sheets in the lower part of the quarterdecl bulwarks, and a third pair for the mainsail tacks at the level of the forecastle

Two ports for the lombard guns are cut in each quarterdeck bulwark These ports are not fitted with lids, since these were a later invention.

Decoration of the hull

The decoration of the reconstructed *Santa Maria* was deliberately kept to minimum, for reasons of authenticity. The stern transom was pa'

Table 3: SANTA MARIA AS A NAO (MARTINEZ-HIDALGO, 1964 AND 1991–2)

Hull maximum length	29.6m	97ft	7in
Keel length	16.1m	52ft	9½in
Breadth	7.9m	26ft	1in
Depth	3.2m	10ft	7in
Light displacement	104.6 tons		
Load displacement	223.8 tons		
Mainmast height from keel to truck	26.6m	87ft	3½in
Mainmast height upon deck	15.9m	52ft	2½in
Foremast height upon forecastle	9.7m	31ft	9½in
Mizzen mast height upon quarterdeck	10.4m	34ft	3½in
Main yard length	16.4m	53ft	9½in
Mainsail area	165.9sq m	1786sq ft	
Foresail area	40.0sq m	430.7sq ft	
Topsail area	18.1sq m	194.9sq ft	
Spritsail area	18.3sq m	197sq ft	
Mizzen sail area	27.5sq m	296sq ft	

white, as were the insides of the bulwarks and stanchions of the main deck, quarterdeck and poop. The quarterdeck and poop bulkheads of the Martinez-Hidalgo replica were decorated with green arches, and white points as shown in the *Llibre del Consolat y dels Fets maritims*, 1502 edition. Red paint was used on the wales and vertical futtock riders. The planking of the hull below the waterline was protected from barnacles and shipworm by a coat of tar and tallow. The freeboard planks were treated with whale or fish oil or a combination of the two.

Forecastle bitt, capstan and anchors
An important characteristic of the bow is the great arch which gives access to the lower forecastle (*tilla*). A significant feature of this area is a large curved beam running athwartships from bulwark to bulwark, with its ends projecting through the side planking. This beam also features in the Mataró nao, but clear evidence of its function is provided by the drawing on the cover of the *Llibre del Consolat y dels Fets maritims*: it served as a large bitt, notably for belaying the anchor cable.

A kind of vertical capstan is shown on the original plans, but this was modified in the models as built, being replaced by a type of capstan which could be used both on board and ashore, for working heavy gear or for careening.

The anchors are based on those used in the reconstructions of both Fernández-Duro and Guillén, with the addition of a ring in the crown for the fish pendant used to buoy them. The ship carried seven anchors, four forward (two of them lashed to the catheads), two grapnels also stowed forward, plus a reserve anchor called a *fornaresa* stowed in the hold. The bower anchors weighed 460kg (1013lb) and each had hemp cables of 80 fathoms length. The grapnels were 46 and 92kg (100lb and 200lb) respectively. The spare sheet anchor was heavier.

Rigging
The catalogue of sails of the *Santa Maria* deduced from Columbus's logbook (see page 12) has been accepted by the authors of all the previous reconstructions. There are, however, some small differences in interpretation which are worth noting.

The most powerful sail, providing most of the drive for the ship, was the mainsail. In the Martinez-Hidalgo reconstruction its area is 166sq m (1,790sq ft). The foresail is the next largest, equal to about a quarter of the mainsail in area.

All sails are made of canvas about 60cm (2ft) wide sewn in the traditional manner with two seams. The mainsail is strengthened with sewn horizontal strips 60cm (2ft) apart. This feature is based on the ships in the Pizzigani Chart of 1367 in the Biblioteca Reale, Parma, Italy. Later evidence is provided by an illuminated letter of the manuscript *Les Bones Costums e els Bons Usatges de la Mar* by Joan Crespi in the Archivo Municipal of Valencia.

The function of the foresail, spritsail and mizzen sail was more that of balancing the rig and helping to keep a steady course. All three sails were made with vertical seams only.

The use of bonnets has been noted above in the description of the other rigs; the connection between mainsail and bonnet is as follows. The upper bonnet carries lacings whose loops pass through the eyelets on the foot of the mainsail and through each other to form a chain lacing. Every tenth loop and its corresponding eyelet is marked with one of the letters A, M, G or P, an abbreviation of *Ave Maria Gratia Plena*. Columbus's crewmen matched the letters as the bonnet was attached, so there was no mistake in hauling the sails out.

Following the old tradition of decorating sails (characteristic of later Roman ships and also Viking and Hanseatic vessels), it was decided to paint red crosses on the topsail, foresail and mainsail.

The only point where complete agreement was not reached is the shape of the topsail, which Fernández-Duro and Guillén took from the Diego Brochero Chart, drawn 40 years after Columbus's voyage. This topsail was trapezoidal, with its sheets reeving through blocks at the yardarms of the mainyard, then through blocks under the top and down to the deck. Martinez-Hidalgo followed drawings by the Venetian artist Carpaccio and those of a Portuguese chart of the early sixteenth century. The sail, about 18sq m (194sq ft in area) is set on a light yard supported by a single flag pole without shrouds, which were not used at that time. The sail is sheeted at the rim of the top. Later, when the topmast became of greater importance and was supported by shrouds and stays, the topsail was certainly trapezoidal, of greater size and sheeted to the yardarms.

The rigging and spars are typical of the Spanish naos of the period, as far as can be established. The very large, heavy mainmast has a diameter of 65cm (25½in) at the partners and 40cm (15⅘in) at the hounds, and is reinforced by rope wooldings and wedges which reach to half the height of the poop above the main deck. The mainmast is supported by six pairs of shrouds, set up to the channels with deadeyes, lanyards and chainplates, as shown in the carrack painted by the Flemish artist known as W A in 1475.

A heavy main stay is rigged from the top to the stem, and secured by deadeyes and lanyards at the gammoning of the stem knee.

Ratlines placed on the mainmast shrouds are based on early sources such as the seal of the City of Danzig (dating from 1400); Martinez-Hidalgo disagreed with Morison's view that ratlines were not in use as early as 1492. The foremast shrouds do not have ratlines, but there is a rope ladder to allow access to the mast top.

The foremast shrouds and the tackles which support the mizzen mast are set up not to channels but to the waterways, using blocks rather than deadeyes and lanyards.

The main yard is hoisted by a double tye which reeves through blocks at the yardarms, at the outer thirds of the yard and under the top.

The mainyard and foreyard are each of two pieces, lashed together. The spritsail and topsail yards are of one piece only. The spritsail yard runs along the bowsprit as in the previous replicas.

The mizzen sail, as for all lateen sails, was set to a two-piece yard which crossed its mast at about 40 degrees. Martinez-Hidalgo did not believe there was a boomkin at the poop as fitted in the other reconstructions; he believed the mizzen mast was stepped further forward, and that the sheet of the mizzen sail ran to the taffrail.

The bowsprit does not have a bobstay, as was fitted in the Fernández-Duro replica. It is stepped at the side of the foremast, and lashed to it. A light foremast stay reeves through a block at the forward end of the bowsprit and belays inboard.

The rim of the top has a strong leather-lined frame, with stanchions and arched panels between. Note that there are some differences in its external appearance between the plans and the reconstructed vessel.

All running rigging is made from hemp and the standing rigging is the same, tarred. In Columbus's time a kind of vegetable fibre referred to in Spain as *esparto* was also used for rigging, though only in light gear and in anchor cables of larger diameter, and for use in fresh water where hemp rotted quickly.

Flags

The *Santa Maria* flew the flag of Castille and Leon, quartered white and red, with yellow castles on the red and red lions crowned in yellow on the white. This same flag can be seen at the top of the mainmasts of the Castilian naos in Juan de la Cosa's chart. The mizzen mast carried the insignia given to the fleet as a special distinction, a white flag with a green cross in its centre, and on either side an F and a Y crowned (the initials of King Ferdinand and the Queen Isabella, the Catholic monarchs).

The Admiral's flag was a standard of red damask with a painted image of Christ crucified on one side and one of the Holy Virgin on the other, mounted on a lance, with gold cords and tassels. This standard was kept in the Admiral's cabin, for use only on solemn occasions. It was carried on the starboard side on landing, and in the ceremonies of taking possession of territory. The pennant was hoisted on the mizzen mast.

On the starboard side of the quarterdeck was the blue ensign with golden anchors of the Capitan General de la Mar Oceano, and a jack with the arms of Columbus was hoisted at the poop. These latter flags were not carried by Columbus on his first voyage; they represent honours granted to him after the Discovery.

THE CARAVELS

The *Diccionario de la Real Academia de la Lengua Española* defines the caravel as a vessel 'very swift, long and narrow, with only one deck, a beak at the prow and a flat poop, with three masts for lateen sails and some with yards for square sails on the main and foremasts'.

According to the *Encyclopedia of Ships and Seafaring* edited by Peter Kemp (Stanford Maritime Press), caravels became the preferred ships of explorers of the late fifteenth and sixteenth centuries, mainly because they were small, roomy, easy to handle and drew so little water that they could approach unknown shores with little danger of running aground.

The caravel was first employed by the Portuguese around 1440 on voyages of discovery to the western African coasts, but the oldest caravels were those used by Portuguese fishermen from the middle of the thirteenth century. The name 'caravel' had been given to certain vessels which appeared in that century in documents such as the *Foral* of Vilanova d Gaia (1255), and notes in *Os descovrimentos Portugueses* defined them a ships with high sides, lateen rigged and fitted with one, two, three or ever four masts. Their capacity was about 100 tons. In the fifteenth century the reached 150, and up to 180 tons.

Lopez de Mendoça provided documentary evidence of the history and development of the caravel up to the beginning of the sixteenth century. The characteristic vessel which emerges from his work is a swift ship of les than 200 tons, with one, two, three or even four masts, exclusively lateen rigged. Nevertheless, extant contemporary documents reveal many differences in vessels falling within the definition of the type. Quirino d. Fonseca, for example, records no fewer than twenty-four different types o bow, all taken from nautical charts, manuscript illustrations and other doc uments, in his *A Caravela Portuguesa*.

Certain characteristic features can, however, be identified. Caravels a had a continuous main deck and no forecastle, but rather a small covered space at the prow known as the *tilla*. The hull was relatively narrow, th transom square, and the rudder hung on the sternpost, with the tiller enter ing the space under the quarterdeck through an opening known as th *limera*. The gunwales were not always bulwarks; sometimes they consisted simply of stanchions with a handrail. Some of the larger caravels had cabin or *chupeta* at the quarterdeck, with a poop deck or *toldilla* above. Th Guillén reconstruction of the *Santa Maria* represents a typical armed car avel, known as a *carabela de armada*, distinguished by a top on th mainmast.

The simplicity of these ships as fishing vessels is evident from drawings o single-masted caravels which accompany the signatures of Spanish fisher men in documents kept in the Archivo de Indias in Seville.

The lateen rig was dominant for caravels in the Mediterranean. It i recorded that King Joao II of Portugal promoted the belief that stron; currents and contrary winds impeded the return of square sailed ships from the west coast of Africa, and that only lateen rigged caravels, then a exclusive Portuguese type, would be able to trade with the newly explored lands. His confidence in a secure Portuguese monopoly was soon shaken however. Caravels operating beyond the Mediterranean were increasingl modified to carry a square sail on the foremast and the mainmast, with spritsail and a lateen mizzen, or a mixed rig adapted to the prevailing winds

It may be that the square rig for caravels originated in Spain, wher square-rigged versions of the vessel appeared in the second quarter of th fifteenth century, and where they survived until the beginning of the six teenth. As in the case of the *Niña* and *Pinta*, lateen-rigged caravels wer frequently converted to square rig, even by the Portuguese, as the advant ages of square sails became apparent.

The general arrangement of Portuguese and Spanish lateen-rigged car avels, as well as those with square sails and a lateen mizzen, is shown i illustrations on the chart of Juan de la Cosa (circa 1500). Vessels illustrated include three Portuguese caravels of two and three masts off the Cape o Good Hope, several lateen-rigged versions off the coasts of Ethiopia and Arabia, and two Spanish caravels (one with a top), both lateen rigged.

Further fine illustrations of lateen-rigged caravels appear in the chart o Pedro Reynel (dating from 1516) now in the Bibliotheque National i Paris.

Early Portuguese records mentioning caravels frequently also refer t other ship types, including *barcas*, *barineis*, *urcas* and *fustas*; none of thes

Table 4: **THE CARAVEL NIÑA, SQUARE RIGGED**

Hull maximum length	21.4m	70ft 2½in
Keel length	15.5m	51ft
Breadth	6.2m	20ft 7in
Depth	2.0m	6ft 6in
Light displacement	48.6 tons	
Load displacement	100.3 tons	
Mainmast height upon deck	16.0m	52ft 6in
Foremast height upon forecastle	9.8m	32ft 1in
Mizzen mast height upon quarterdeck	8.1m	26ft 8½in
Mainsail area	115.7sq m	1245.8sq ft
Foresail area	40.6sq m	437.2sq ft
Mizzen sail area	22.5sq m	243sq ft

Table 5: **THE CARAVEL PINTA**

Hull maximum length	22.7m	74ft 7in
Keel length	16.1m	52ft 9½in
Breadth	6.6m	21ft 7in
Depth	2.2m	7ft 2½in
Light displacement	51.6 tons	
Load displacement	115.6 tons	
Mainmast length upon deck	15.7m	51ft 8½in
Foremast height upon forecastle	9.1m	30ft
Mizzen mast height upon quarterdeck	8.1m	26ft 8½in
Mainsail area	120.0sq m	1292sq ft
Foresail area	43.2sq m	465.1sq ft
Mizzen sail area	23.4sq m	252.2sq ft

types survives in the chronicles of the voyages of discovery. Only the caravel, clearly an exceptional vessel, ensured its place in history as a recognisable ship type.

The *Niña* was owned by Juan Niño of Moguer (in Huelva, southern Spain), who took part in the first voyage as her master, under the captain Vicente Yáñez Pinzón of Palos. Her original name was *Santa Clara*, and the name *Niña* ('Little Girl') was an allusion to her owner's surname. She was built in Moguer, on the banks of the Rio Tinto, where Spanish shipwrights competed in skill with the Portuguese of the nearby Algarve.

Columbus himself had a great fondness for the *Niña*, and sailed some 25,000 miles in her. He eventually became her half-owner, and captained the ship himself on the second voyage.

The last record of the *Niña* relates to a voyage she made to the so-called Coast of Pearls (modern Venezuela) in 1501. This coast had been explored by Juan de la Cosa (the *Santa Maria*'s owner and master on Columbus's first voyage) and Alonso de Hojeda in 1499. The ship's part in this enterprise has been investigated by Alice Gould, to whom is due the credit for the most reliable study of Columbus's crews.

The *Pinta* belonged to Christóbal Quintero of Palos, who also accompanied his ship on Columbus's first voyage. Her captain was Martin Alonso Pinzón of Palos, and her master his cousin Francisco Martin Pinzón.

In his reconstruction of the caravels which accompanied Columbus, Martinez-Hidalgo was careful to take into account the lines and characteristics of related ship types which are more fully documented. The lines of the xebecs on display in the Museu Maritim at Barcelona were particularly informative, given that the xebec and the caravel are closely related vessels. Notable features in common are the relation between length and breadth, the run of the planking at the bow and the stern and the extraordinary ability of both types to sail close to the wind. Similarly, the main frame and stern of the baghala and the sambuk, both of which are similar to the later caravels, were taken into consideration. It was also necessary to take note of the illustrations of two-masted lateen caravels on the chart of Juan de la Cosa, which show a square tuck at the stern with diagonal planking.

Martinez-Hidalgo used the method described in the *Livro Nautico*, a unique Portuguese source for the study of caravels from somewhat later than Columbus's time, for calculating the dimensions of the reconstructions from the tonnage of the original *Niña* and *Pinta*. Miguel de Cuneo, who returned from Cuba in 1494, recorded the tonnage of the *Niña* as about 60 tons; other data in the *Recolta Colombina* suggest that she embarked some 51 tons of cargo and supplies. The hold capacity of the somewhat larger *Pinta* was about 60 tons. The proportions suggested by the *Livro Nautico* are breadth 2.30 times depth in the hold, keel length 2.40 times breadth, and length overall 3.33 times breadth.

The *Pinta* replica has an extended quarterdeck and *tilla*, together with raised bulwarks at the bow; it is quite clear that the design and construction of caravels was no more standardised than that of any other vessel at the time, and these features of the *Pinta* replica indicate some of the more obvious modifications for ocean-going examples of the type.

The frames for the reconstructed caravels comprised two futtocks, joined at the keel and reinforced by floor timbers, with the whole structure secured by a keelson. The main frame on the *Niña* is some 50cm (1ft 8in) forward of the centre point of the keelson, and the disposition of the frames follows a traditional scheme probably dating from Columbus's time; the space between frames is 60cm (about 1ft 11½in).

The external planking of both caravels was reinforced by external riders. On the *Niña* there are six such riders, running from 30cm (about 1ft) below the single wale (and mortised into it) up to the gunwale, with a seventh rider level with the forward edge of the quarterdeck extending right up to the cap rail. The Pinta has six such riders, of which the two aftermost run up to the level of the quarterdeck rail.

The camber of the *Niña*'s main deck is 63cm (about 2ft) and the sheer 75cm (2ft 5½). The deck planks are 20cm (about 8in) wide and laid parallel to the centreline. Two hatches are fitted, the main hatch in the waist with an area of some 2sq m and the other beneath the quarterdeck and somewhat smaller. The quarterdeck is 1.65m (5ft 5in) above the level of the main deck at the waist.

The hull of the *Niña* is without hawse holes, but both replica caravels have openings in the sides for the sheets and tacks of their square sails. Both are fitted with a boomkin at the stern to take the mizzen sheet.

The *Niña* has no channels, and the *Pinta* has channels for the main shrouds only. The normal method of supporting the masts on medieval ships of lateen rig was tackles on the waterways which could be released on the leeward side as necessary to allow free movement to the sail. It is possible that the rerigging of both ships from lateen to square sails would have necessitated the fitting of channels for the mainmast, but none of the models of this type of caravel in the Museu Maritim have channels, and the conversion of the *Niña* anyway took place once the voyage was already underway.

The rerigging of the *Niña* with square sails was nonetheless a major operation. The mizzen mast was moved to the prow to serve as a foremast, and a bowsprit was set up to take the bowlines of the foresail. Parts of the lateen yard were shortened and converted into yards for the square sails. The mainmast was moved slightly aft, and a small mizzen mast was installed on the quarterdeck and provided with a lateen sail.

Neither caravel has a top, a spritsail or a topsail. The mainsail is fitted with a bonnet, but not the foresail (the area of the foresail was somewhat greater than one quarter that of the main, bonnet included).

As in the *Santa Maria*, the capstan fitted to the original caravels for handling the anchor (and, when necessary, for raising the main yard) could probably be unshipped and used ashore to assist in beaching the vessel. The reconstructed capstans are designed with this in mind.

BIBLIOGRAPHY

Brâs de Oliveira, Joâo *Os Navios de Vasco da Gama* Imprenta Nacional, Lisbon (1971)

Carbonell, Laureano 'La Coca, nave del Medioevo' *Revista de Historia Naval* No 15, Madrid (1986)

Comision del V Centenario *Reconstruccion de las Naves del V Centenario* Madrid (1989)

Concas, Victor M *La Nao Histórica 'Santa Maria' en 1892 y 1893* Imprenta Alemana, Madrid (1914)

Culver, Henry B and Nance, Morton 'A contemporary Fifteenth Century Ship' *The Mariner's Mirror* Vol XV (1929)

Chocano Iglesias, Guadalupe *Naves del Descubrimiento: La 'Santa Maria', la 'Pinta' y la 'Niña'* Museo Naval, Madrid (1985)

Da Fonseca, Quirino *A Caravela Portuguesa e a Prioridade Tecnica das Navegaçoes Henriquinas* Imprenta da Universidade, Coimbra (1934)

Fernandez, Manuel *Livro das Traças da Carpintaria* Biblioteca da Ajuda Lisbon (1616); facsimile edition by the Museu de Marinha, Lisbon

Fernández-Duro, Cesáreo 'La nao *Santa Maria* en 1892' *Memoria de la Comisión Arqueológica Ejecutiva* Madrid (1892)

Guillén y Tato, Julio F *La Carabela 'Santa Maria'* Imprenta del Ministerio de Marina, Madrid (1927)

Martinez-Hidalgo, José M *A bordo de la 'Santa Maria'* Diputación de Barcelona (1961)

Las Naves de Colón Editorial Cadí, Barcelona (1969)

Nogueira da Brito 'Caravelas, Naus e Galés de Portugal' *Enciclopedia pela Imagem* Livraria Lello Lda, Porto

Pastor, Xavier 'La elección de un motivo y las distintas versiones de la *Santa Maria* de Colón' *Revista Yate y Motonaútica* Barcelona (May, June, July, August 1977)

Pastor, Xavier (with Laureano Carbonell and Jose M Martinez-Hidalgo) *La Coca de Mataró: Morfología del Ex-voto y la Construcción de su Réplica* Cámara Oficial de Comercio, Barcelona (1986)

Pastor, Xavier *A replica of the Nao Catalana (Catalan Vessel) of 1450 in the Prins Hendrik Museum, Rotterdam, built in Spain in 1985* Lecture read by Leo M Akveld at the VI International Congress of Maritime Museums Amsterdam & Rotterdam (1987)

Taviani, Paolo Emilio *Los Viajes de Colón: El Gran Descubrimiento* Instituto Geográfico Agostini, Novara (1984)

Varela, Consuelo *Cristobal Colón: Textos y Documentos Completos* Alianza Editorial (U), Madrid, (1982)

Winter, Heinrich *Die Katalanische Nao von 1450* Robert Loef, Magdeburg (1956)

Die Kolumbusschiffe von 1492 Hinstorf Verlag, Rostock (1968)

The Photographs

1. A fine starboard quarter view of the
Fernández-Duro replica of the *Santa Maria*.
Conway Picture Library

2. The launch of the Fernández-Duro replica of the *Santa Maria* as a nao at La Carraca Shipyard, near Cadiz, on 26 June 1892.

3. The Fernández-Duro *Santa Maria* off Huelva, in the south of Spain; Christopher Columbus set sail on his first voyage from this area.
Reproduced from the Memoria de la Comision Arqueológica, *Madrid, 1892*

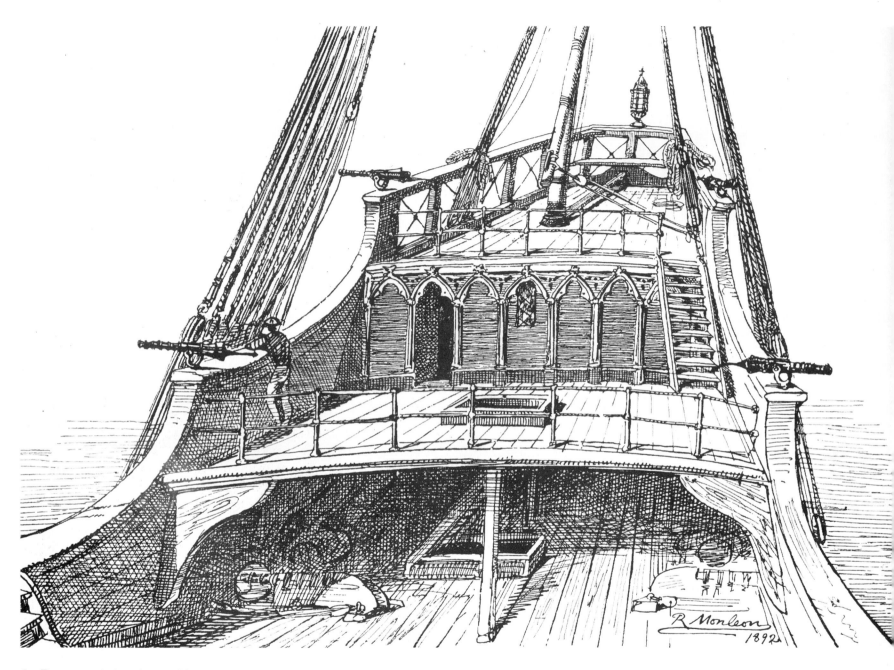

4. The quarterdeck and poop of the
Fernández-Duro *Santa Maria*.
Drawing by R Monleon, 1892

5. The *Santa Maria* as a caravel, as reconstructed by Guillén in 1927, off Huelva.
Manuel Ripoll collection

6. The Guillén *Santa Maria* under repair at La Carraca Shipyard, near Cadiz. *Xavier Pastor, 1940.*

7. The windlass of Guillén's *Santa Maria*. *Museu Maritim, Barcelona*

8. The hold of the Guillén *Santa Maria*.
Museu Maritim, Barcelona

9. Lombard cannon and the firebox under
the Guillén *Santa Maria*'s quarterdeck.
Museu Maritim, Barcelona

25

10. A detail of one of the two naos in the altarpiece *La Vida de Santa Ursula*, painted by Joan de Reixach in 1450. Formerly in the Church of Cubellas, Lleida, the painting is now in the Museu d'Art de Catalunya in Barcelona. The curved transverse beam for securing the anchor cables is visible through the arch of the forecastle. The planking below the forecastle is clinker fashion, in contrast to the carvel-built hull. Note that the shrouds have no ratlines, although the man seen climbing to the top in the upper right corner of the picture seems to be using them; possibly the ratlines were missed when restoration work was done.
Xavier Pastor

11. This nao from the cover of the *Llibre del Consolat y dels Fets Maritims* (1502 edition) shows clearly the large horizontal bitt under the forecastle, in the space known as the *tilla*.

2. The hull of the model known as the *Nao de Mataró*, dated 1450 and possibly an ex-voto, which is said to have been on view at the Ermita de San Simon, in the coastal town of that name. The Mataró nao is now in the Prins Hendrik Maritiem Museum in Rotterdam.
Xavier Pastor collection

13. The only part clinker built on the Catalan nao was below the forecastle. This feature was reproduced by Martinez-Hidalgo in his version of the *Santa Maria*, as shown in this detail of the model in the Museu Maritim, Barcelona.
Xavier Pastor

14. A parrel on the Mataró ex-voto.
Xavier Pastor

15. Tackles supporting the mainmast on the Mataró model in the Prins Hendrik Maritiem Museum, Rotterdam.
Xavier Pastor

16. A replica of the Mataró model of a Catalan nao, built by Xavier Pastor after research in the Prins Hendrik Maritiem Museum at Rotterdam in 1985. The work was sponsored by the Camara de Comercio of Barcelona, and the model was offered to the Museu Maritim in that city. *Xavier Pastor*

17. The collection of the Victoria and Albert Museum in London includes a Moorish bowl from the early fifteenth century, manufactured in Màlaga, Spain, whose decoration is a three-masted nao of a type similar to that represented by the Mataró model. The bulwarks of the forecastle are clinker built, and the structure over the quarterdeck is very similar to that of the Mataró model.

18. A reproduction of the drawing of a nao on the chart of Gracioso Benicasa, dated 1482, in the Biblioteca dell'Università, Bologna, Italy. The sails have squared reinforcements, and other details are also very informative.

19. The same type of reinforcement for the sails can be seen in the chart of the Pizzigani brothers, dating from 1367, more than a century earlier, now in the Biblioteca Palatina in Parma.

20. A reproduction of a drawing of a nao in the *Regimento do Astrolabio e do Quadrante*, the oldest nautical treatise known (dating from 1509). The only known copy is now in the Staatsbibliothek in Munich.

21. A nao under construction in a Venetian shipyard, from the *Peregrinationem in Terram Sanctam* by Bernard von Breydenbach (1495). This work was translated into Spanish by Martín Martínez Dampies and published in 1498. The drawing is reproduced from the article 'La Navegacion en el Mediterráneo en el Siglo XV, época de la Coca de Mataró' by Laureano Carbonell.

22. A detail from the carved altarpiece in the church of San Nicolas at Burgos, Spain (carved between 1480 and 1503), showing a nao. Channels, shrouds with ratlines, and tops are clearly visible.
Drawing by R Monleon

23. Spanish and Portuguese naos from the chart of Juan de la Cosa, *circa* 1500.

24. A woodcut depicting a Spanish ship from 1496.
Museo Naval, Madrid

25. Details such as the tackle at the top, the mainsail bonnets and the rudder are shown clearly in this drawing from *La Vida de Santa Magdalena* by Joan Jofre, published in Valencia in 1505.

26. This bronze relief of the Sacrifice of Jonah by Bellano (dating from 1514) in the Basilica of San Antonio at Padua, Italy, shows clearly the great arch of the forecastle, the horizontal bitt and the clinker-built bulwarks below the forecastle.

27. A reproduction of a drawing of a Flemish carrack by the artist known as W A dating from 1475. The mainmast shrouds have no ratlines, but a Jacob's ladder gives access to the top. The shrouds are secured by heart-shaped deadeyes and lanyards to channels. The Great Arch – as Winter called it – is visible under the forecastle. A large single-piece mizzen yard is supported by bridles

28. In the Atlas attributed to the cartographer Pedro Reinel (1516) in the Bibliothèque National, Paris, there are drawings of three masted lateen Portuguese caravels; this drawing is based on one of them.

29. Lateen caravels drawn beside the signatures of fishermen on a document in the Archivo de Indias, Seville.

30. A four-masted Portuguese caravel from the *Livro Naútico* (late sixteenth century), reproduced from the book *A Caravela Portuguesa* by Quirino da Fonseca.

37

31. A model of the caravel *Niña* before her lateen rig was changed, based on the research of Martinez-Hidalgo.
Museu Maritim, Barcelona

32. A model of the caravel *Pinta*, based on research by Martinez-Hidalgo. *Museu Maritim, Barcelona*

33. The hull of the model of the Martinez-Hidalgo *Niña* under construction. *Museu Maritim, Barcelona*

34. A port bow view of the model of the Martinez-Hidalgo *Niña*, showing the deck layout.
Museu Maritim, Barcelona

The Drawings

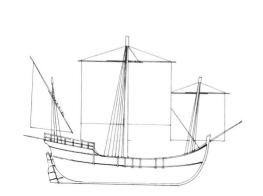 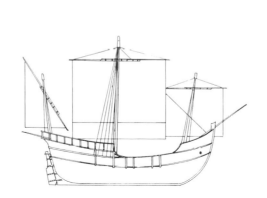 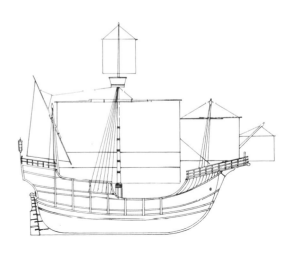

A The Fernández-Duro replica (1892)

A1   HULL PROFILE (1/100 scale)

1. Stem
2. Keel
3. Sternpost
4. Knee
5. Rudder
6. Forecastle bulwark
7. Poop open rail
8. Decoration
9. Channel
10. Wales
11. Futtock riders
12. Anchor
13. Hawse hole
14. Bowsprit
15. Foremast
16. Mainmast
17. Mizzen mast
18. Boomkin

A1

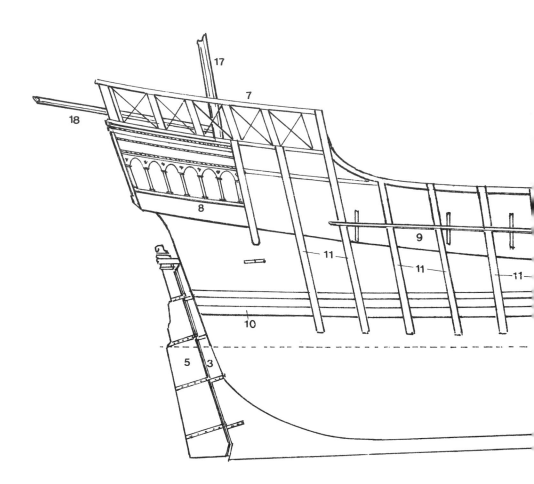

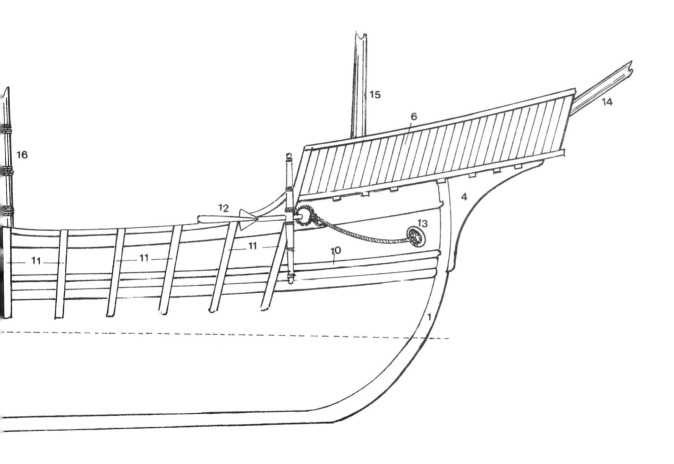

A   The Fernández-Duro replica (1892)

A2   LINES (1/100 scale)

A2/1   Longitudinal lines

1. Waterlines
2. Buttock lines
3. Hold line
4. Main deck line
5. Quarterdeck line
6. Poop deck line
7. Forecastle line

A2/1

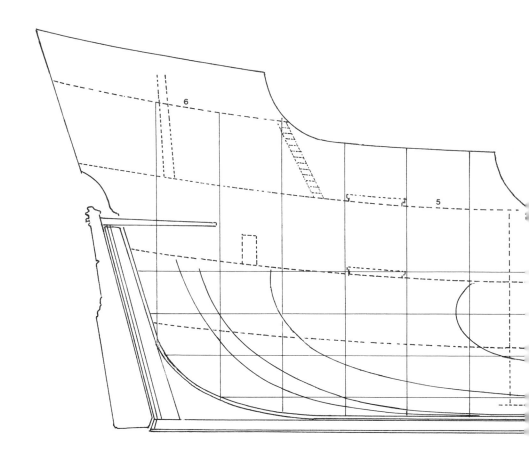

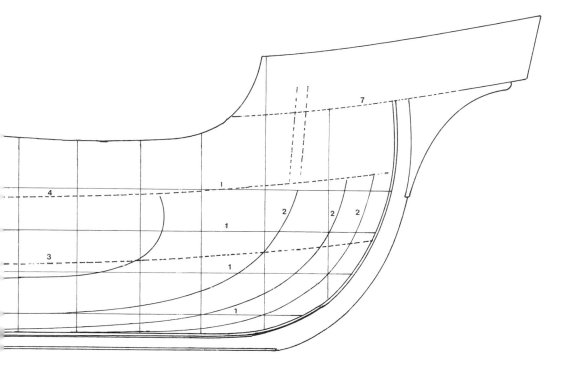

A The Fernández-Duro replica (1892)

A2/2 Body lines

1. Waterlines
2. Bilge diagonals
3. Hold line
4. Main deck line
5. Quarterdeck line
6. Poop deck line
7. Buttocks

A2/2

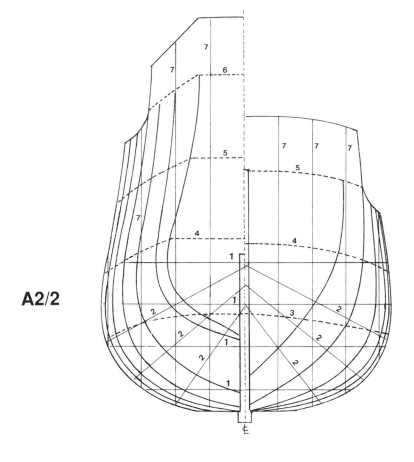

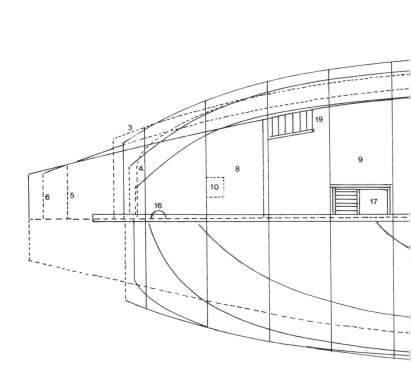

2/3 Breadth lines and deck details

1. Waterlines
2. Bilge diagonals
3. Main deck line
4. Hold line
5. Quarterdeck line
6. Poop deck line
7. Gunwale line
8. Poop deck
9. Quarterdeck
10. Poop deck scuttle
11. Waist
12. Forecastle
13. Foremast
14. Mainmast
15. Pin rack
16. Mizzen mast
17. Hatchway
18. Windlass
19. Ladder
20. Launch
21. Yawl

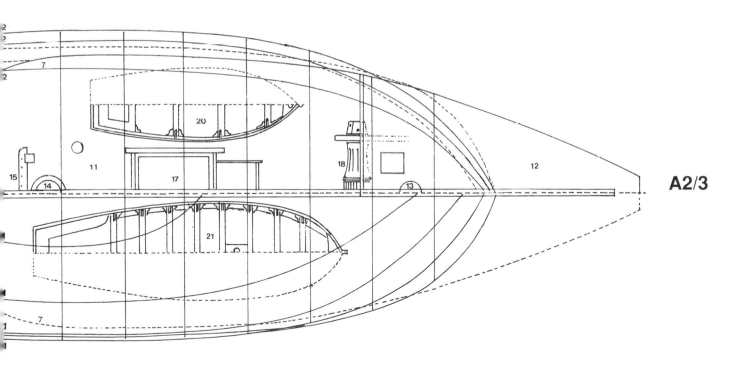

A2/3

B The Guillén replica (1927)

B1   **HULL PROFILE (1/100 scale)**

1.   Stem
2.   Keel
3.   Sternpost
4.   Rudder
5.   Tiller
6.   Wales
7.   Channel
8.   Rail
9.   Futtock rider
10. Anchor
11. Foremast
12. Mainmast
13. Mizzen mast
14. Cleats
15. Bowsprit
16. Boomkin
17. Gunwale

B1

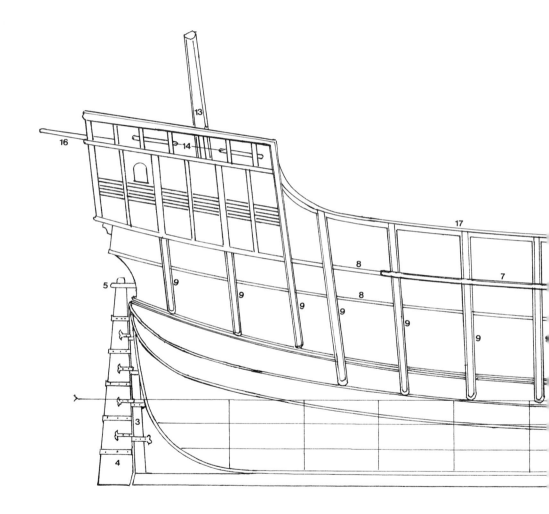

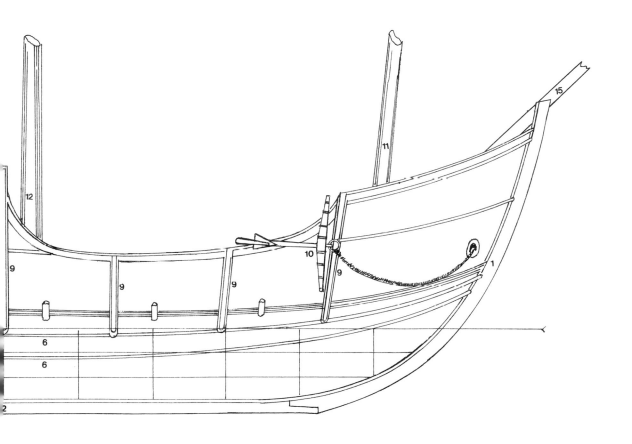

B The Guillén replica (1927)

B2   LINES (1/100 scale)

B2/1 Longitudinal lines

1. Waterlines
2. Buttocks

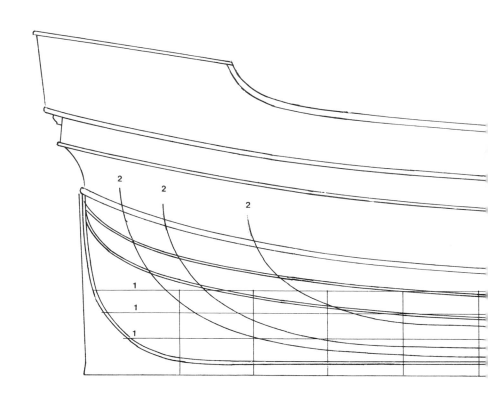

B2/1

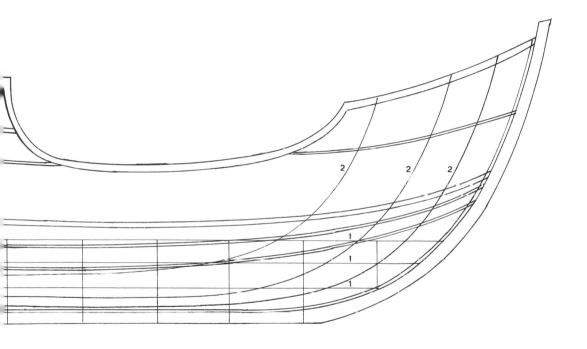

B   The Guillén replica (1927)

B2/2   Body lines

1.   Waterlines
2.   Diagonal lines

B2/2

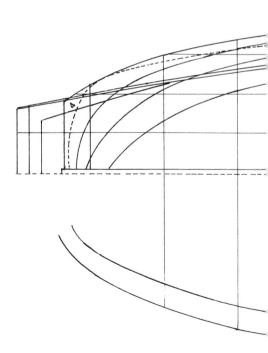

B2/3 **Half breadth lines**

1. Waterlines
2. Diagonal lines
3. Buttocks
4. Main deck line

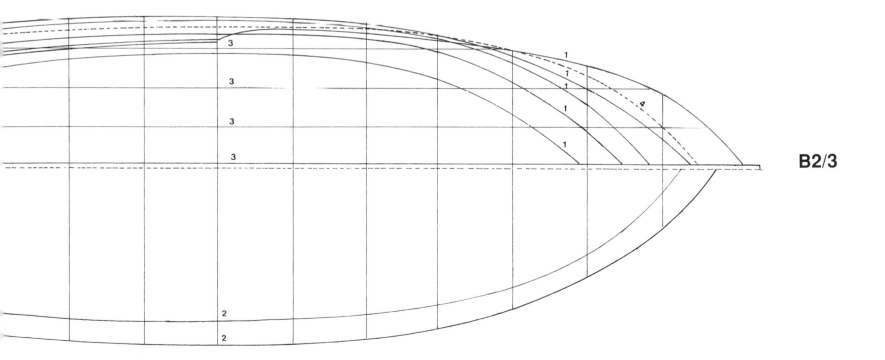

B2/3

53

B The Guillén replica (1927)

B3   DECK PLAN (1/100 scale)

1. Stem
2. Forecastle
3. Main deck
4. Quarterdeck
5. Poop deck
6. Hatchway
7. Ladder
8. Buttock riders
9. Channels
10. Windlass
11. Anchors
12. Foremast
13. Mainmast
14. Mizzen mast

B3

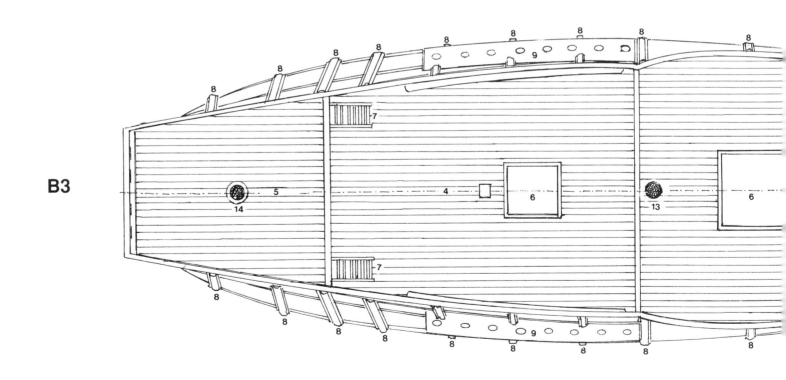

1. Bow elevation
2. Stern elevation
3. Hawse hole
4. Mooring cable hole
5. Tiller port
6. Admiral's cabin window

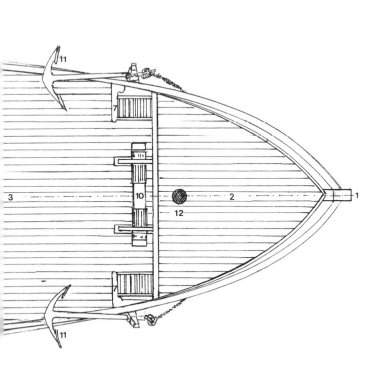

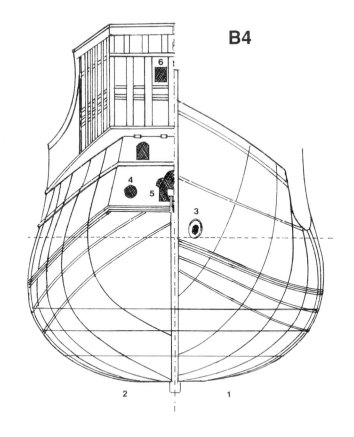

B4

55

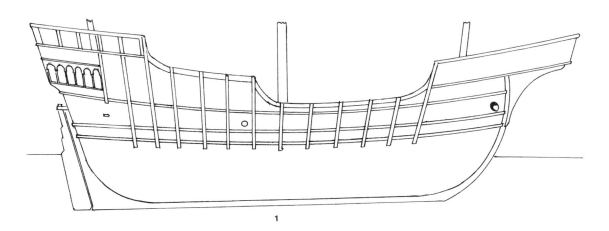

1

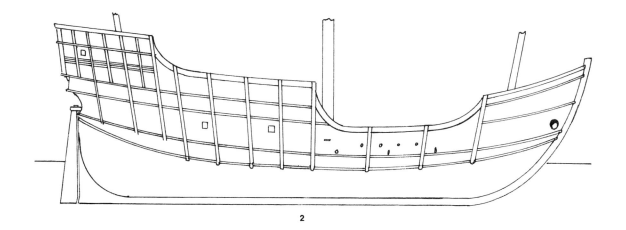

2

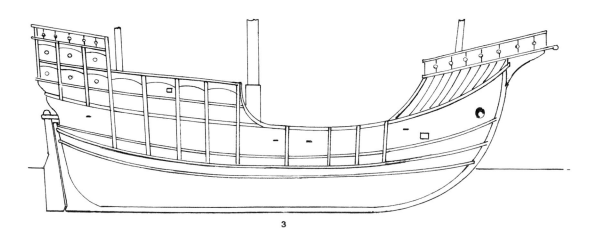

3

C1 **COMPARATIVE HULL PROFILES**
(1/200 scale)

1. *Santa Maria* as a nao by Fernández Duro
2. *Santa Maria* as a caravel by Guillén
3. *Santa Maria* as a nao by Martinez-Hidalgo

C1

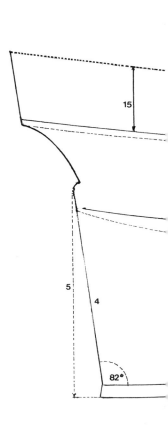

C2   LINES (1/100 scale except as marked)

C2/1   Basic lines of the hull and deck heights

1. Keel
2. Centre of sweep of the stem
3. Vertical part of the stem
4. Sternpost at 82-degree angle
5. Height of the sternpost
6. Height of the main deck at bows
7. Height of the main deck amidships
8. Height of the main deck at the sides
9. Height of the quarterdeck over the main deck
10. Height of the quarterdeck at the sides
11. Height of the space under the forecastle (*tilla*)
12. Level of the forecastle deck amidships
13. Level of the forecastle deck at the sides
14. Level of the rails which support the forecastle structure
15. Height of the poop deck over the quarterdeck

C2/1

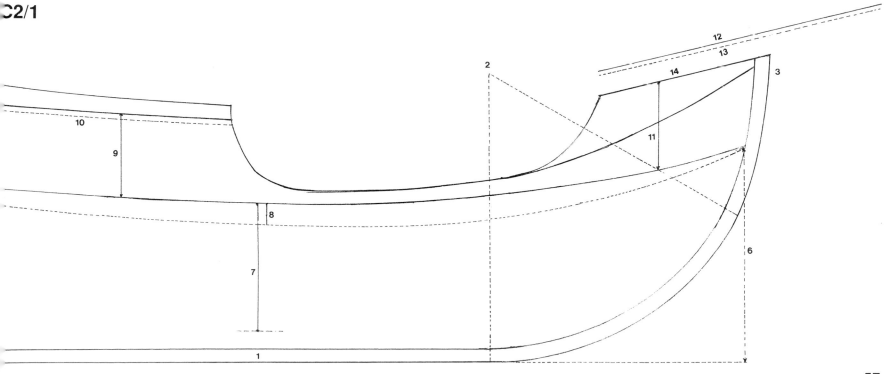

C General arrangement and lines

C2/2

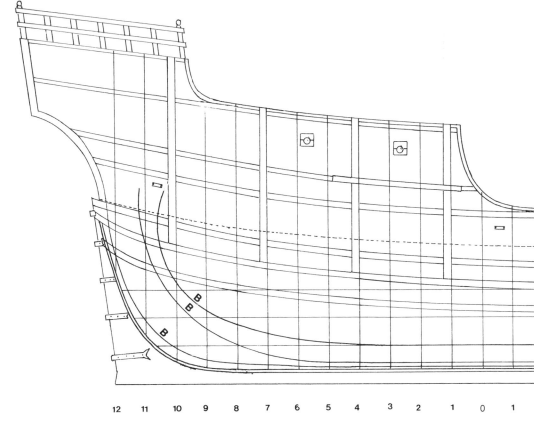

12 11 10 9 8 7 6 5 4 3 2 1 0 1

C2/3

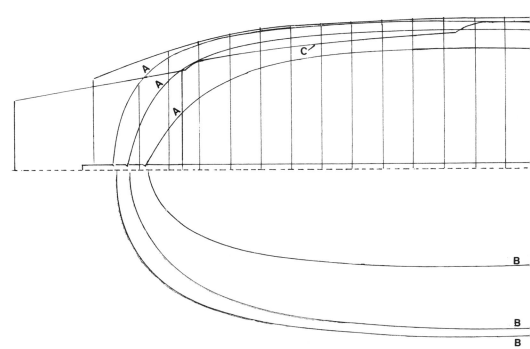

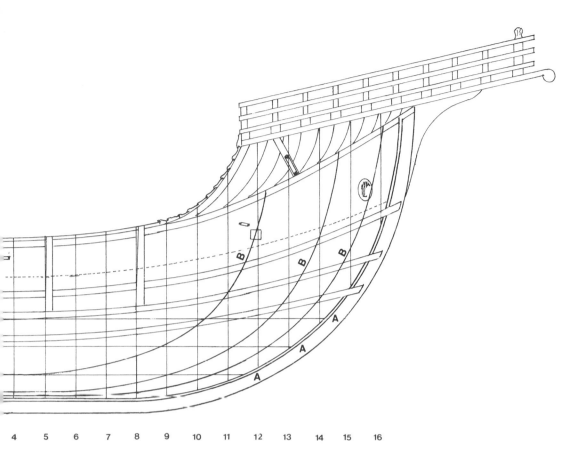

4   5   6   7   8   9   10   11   12   13   14   15   16

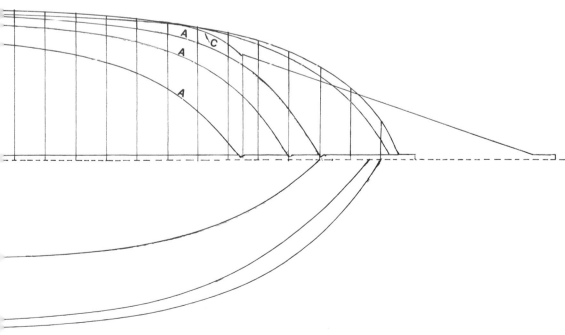

59

C General arrangement and lines

C2/4 Body plan (1/50 scale)

A   Waterlines
B   Bilge diagonals
1–16 Forward sections
0–12 Aft sections

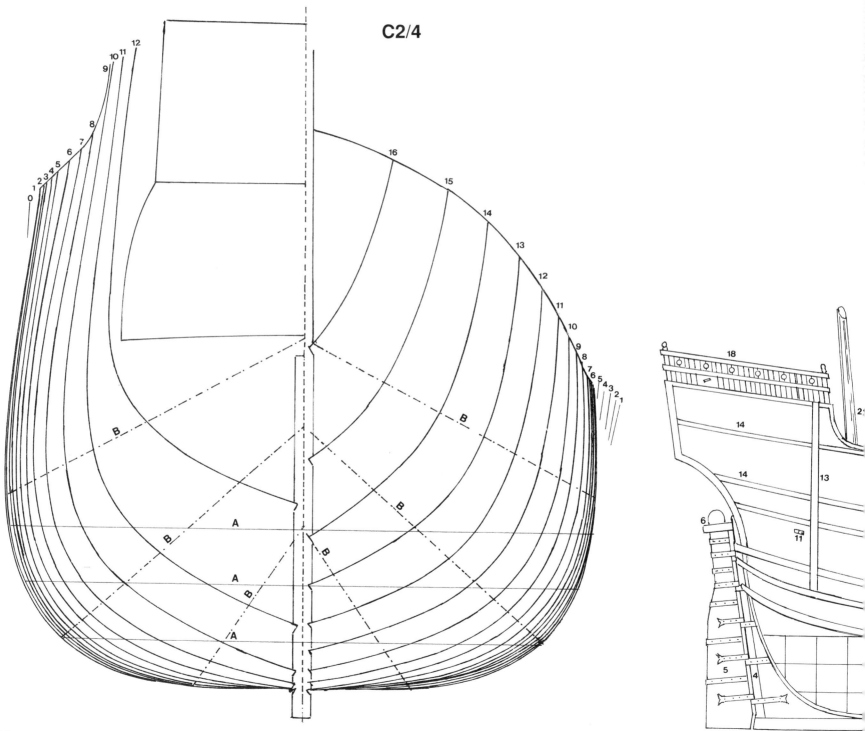

C2/4

HULL PROFILE (1/100 scale)

1. Stempost
2. Knee
3. Keel
4. Sternpost
5. Rudder
6. Tiller
7. Hawse hole
8. Bitt
9. Channel
0. Gun ports
1. Reeving sheave
2. Wales
3. Futtock riders
4. Rail
5. Gunwale
6. Clinker planking
7. Forecastle bulwarks
8. Poop bulwarks
9. Bowsprit
0. Foremast
1. Mainmast
2. Mizzen mast

C3

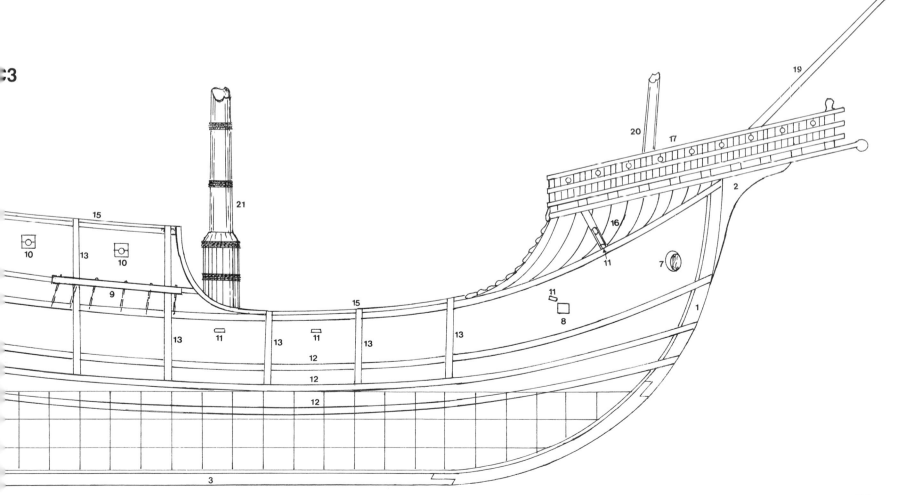

C General arrangement and lines

C4/1

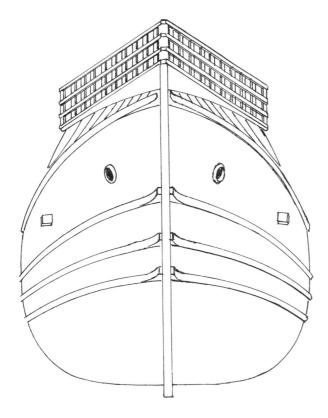

C4/2

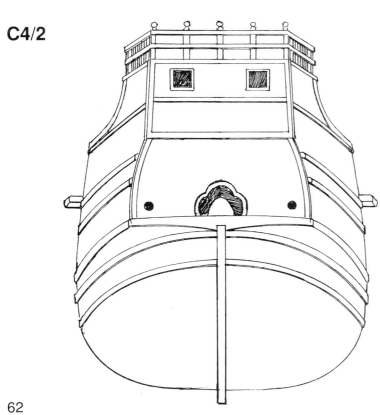

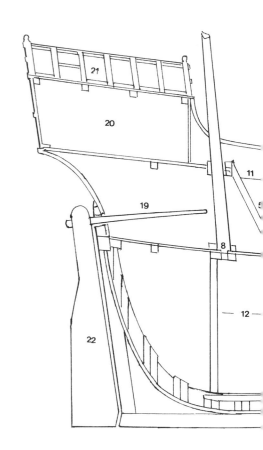

C5 INTERNAL PROFILE OF HULL
(1/100 scale)

1. *Tilla*
2. Bowsprit
3. Foremast
4. Horizontal bitt
5. Ladder
6. Forecastle bulwark
7. Keelson
8. Mast step
9. Mainmast
10. Mainmast wedges
11. Hatchway
12. Hold pillars
13. Stepped pillar
14. Waist
15. Pumps
16. Quarterdeck
17. Bitt
18. Capstan
19. Tiller
20. Admiral's cabin
21. Quarterdeck bulwark
22. Rudder
23. Knee

C5

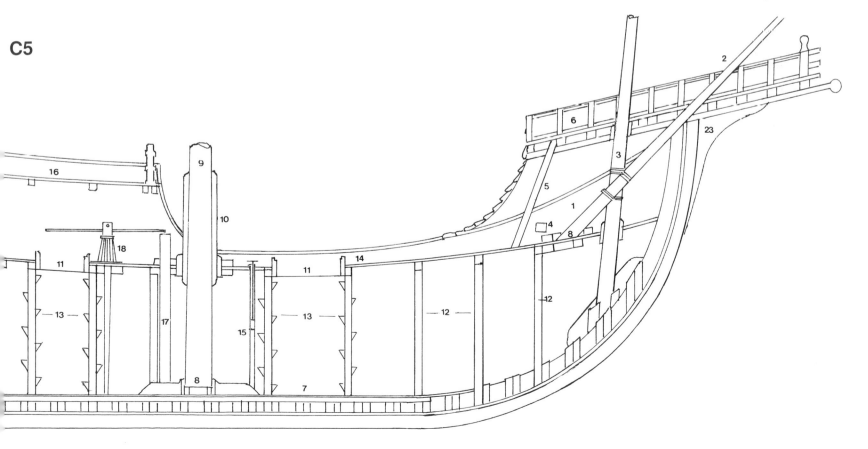

D Hull construction and details

D1 **DISPOSITION OF FRAMES AND RIBBANDS (1/100 scale)**

1. Keel
2. Stem post
3. Sternpost
4. Sternpost heel
5. Keelson
6. Apron
7. False post
8. Floor timbers
9. First futtocks
10. Second futtocks
11. Toptimbers
12. Beam shelf
13. Ribbands

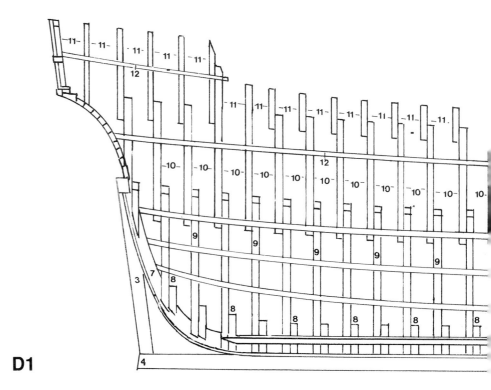

D1

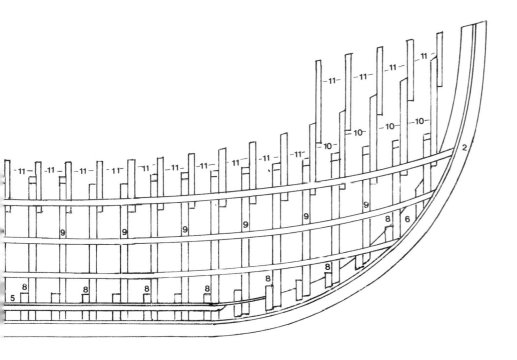

D Hull construction and details

D4 PLAN VIEW OF DECKS
(1/100 scale)

1. Forecastle hatchway
2. Waist hatchway
3. Quarterdeck hatchway
4. Channels
5. Futtock riders
6. Bitt caps
7. Gunwale
8. Foremast
9. Mainmast
10. Mizzen mast
11. Pumps
12. Bowsprit hole

D4

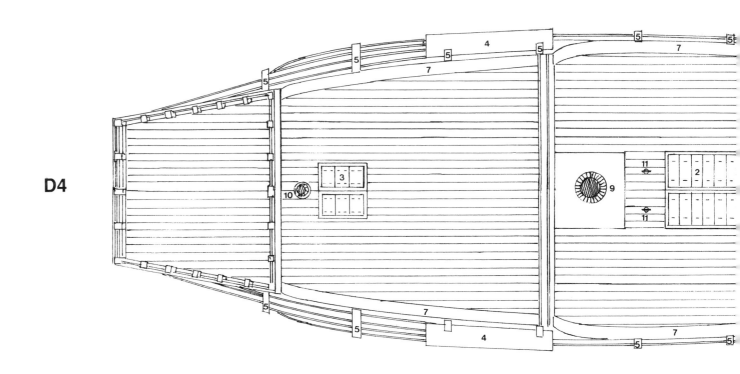

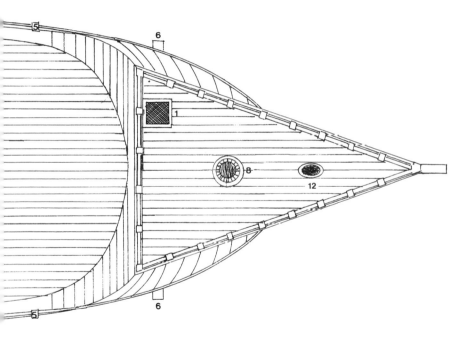

D Hull construction and details

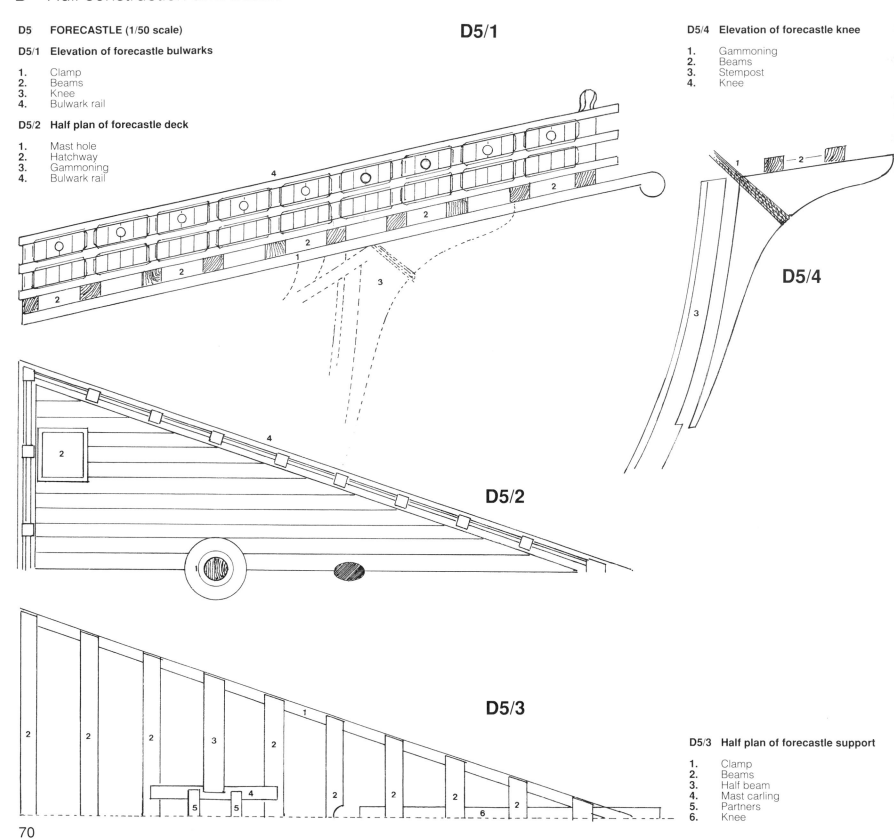

D5   FORECASTLE (1/50 scale)

D5/1   Elevation of forecastle bulwarks

1. Clamp
2. Beams
3. Knee
4. Bulwark rail

D5/2   Half plan of forecastle deck

1. Mast hole
2. Hatchway
3. Gammoning
4. Bulwark rail

D5/4   Elevation of forecastle knee

1. Gammoning
2. Beams
3. Stempost
4. Knee

D5/1

D5/4

D5/2

D5/3

D5/3   Half plan of forecastle support

1. Clamp
2. Beams
3. Half beam
4. Mast carling
5. Partners
6. Knee

D5/5

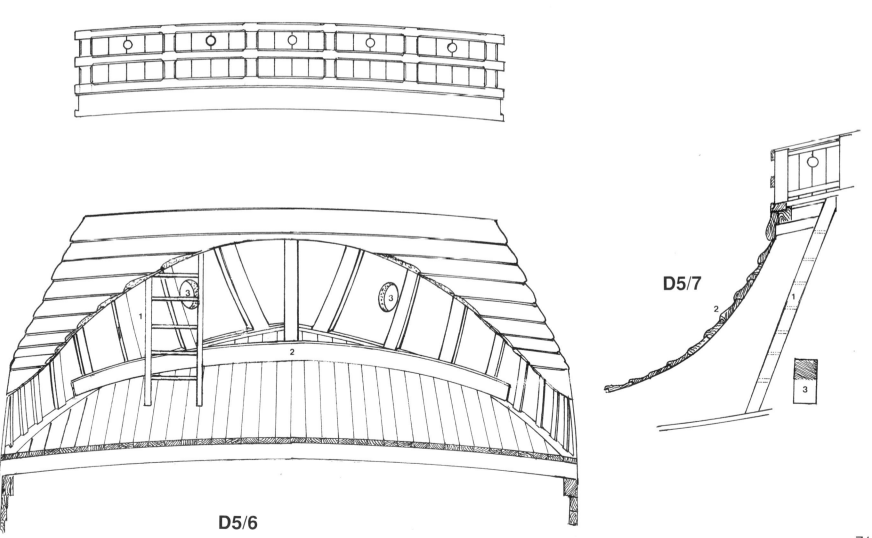

D5/6

D5/7

D   Hull construction and details

D6   QUARTERDECK (1/50 scale)

D6/1   Forward elevation of quarterdeck handrail

D6/2   Section of quarterdeck handrail on the Mataró model (no scale)

D6/3   Perspective view of quarterdeck handrail on the Mataró model (no scale)

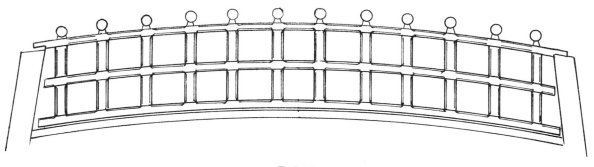

D6/1

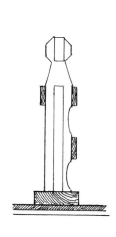

D6/2

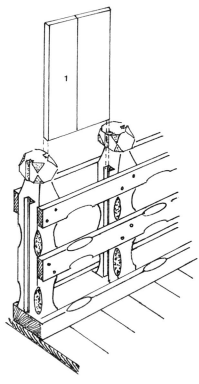

D6/3

D7/1

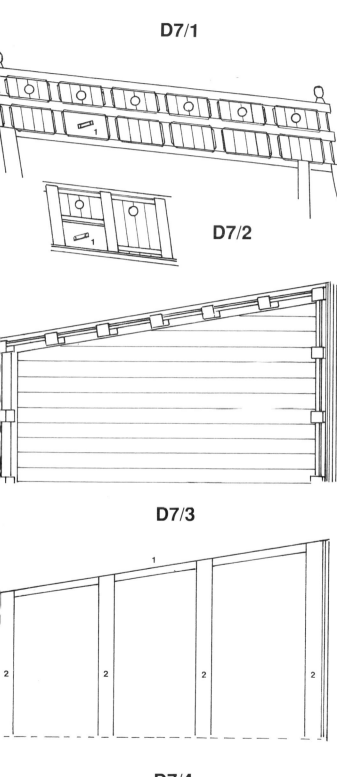

D7/2

D7   **POOP (1/50 scale)**

D7/1   **Side elevation of poop handrail**

1.   Sheave for main brace

D7/2   **Partial internal elevation of poop handrail**

1.   Sheave for main brace

D7/3   **Half plan of poop deck**

D7/4   **Half plan of poop deck support**

1.   Clamp
2.   Beams

D7/5   **After elevation of poop handrail**

1.   Window to admiral's cabin

D7/6   **Forward elevation of poop deck and admiral's cabin**

1.   Poop deck handrail
2.   Ladder
3.   Door to admiral's cabin
4.   Poop deck

D7/3

D7/5

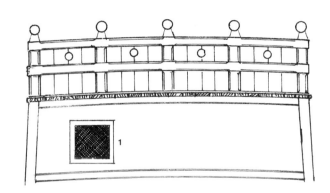

D7/4

D7/6

E   Steering gear

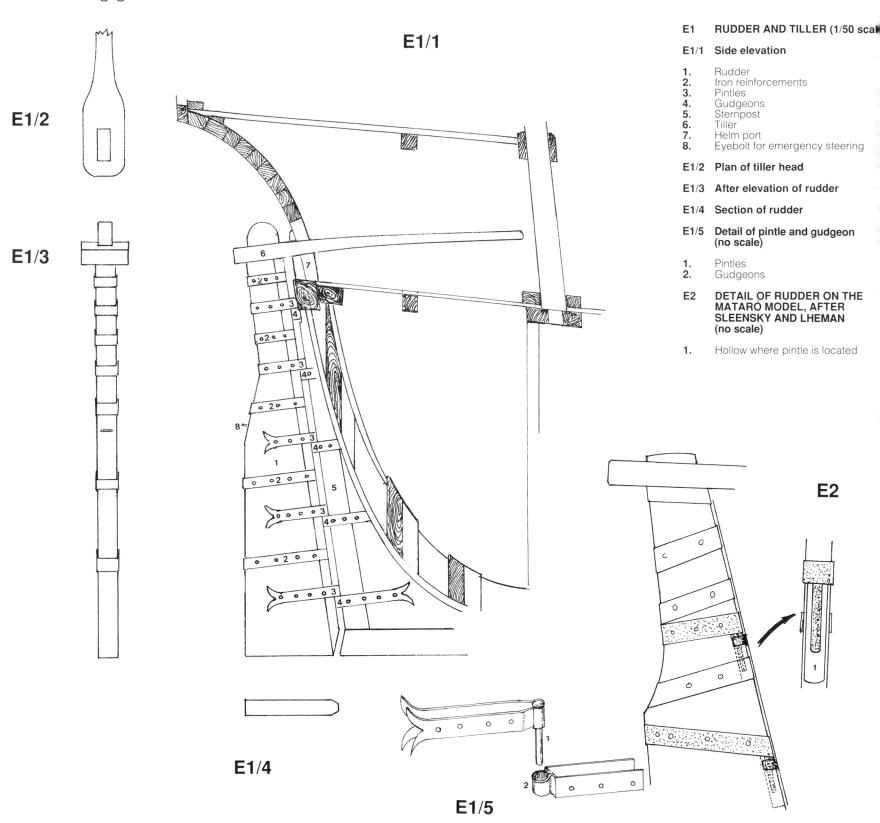

E1/1

E1/2

E1/3

E1/4

E1/5

E2

F Fittings

F1 CAPSTAN (1/15 scale, except as
marked)

F1/1 General arrangement of capstan
(1/50 scale)

1. Main deck
2. Keelson

4. Step
5. Drumhead
6. Bar holes
7. Bars
8. Partners

F1/2 Elevation

. Drumhead
. Holes for bars
. Whelps
. Partners

F1/3 Plan of capstan plant on main
deck

1/4 Reconstruction of caption capable
of use ashore (side elevation)

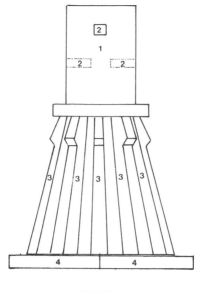

F1/2

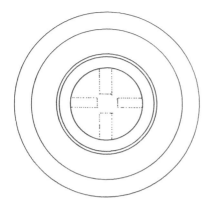

F1/3

F1/1

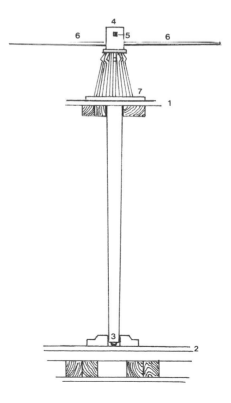

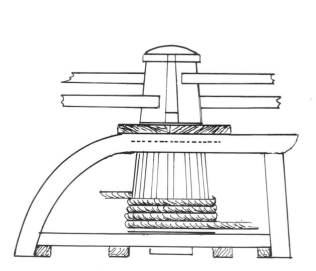

F1/4

F Fittings

F2 WINDLASS (RECONSTRUCTION BY GUILLÉN) (1/40 scale)

F2/1 Plan

1. Carrick bitt
2. Knees
3. Pawl bit
4. Whelps
5. Barrel
6. Slots
7. Drums
8. Bar holes
9. Pawl

F2/2 Forward elevation

F2/3 Side elevation

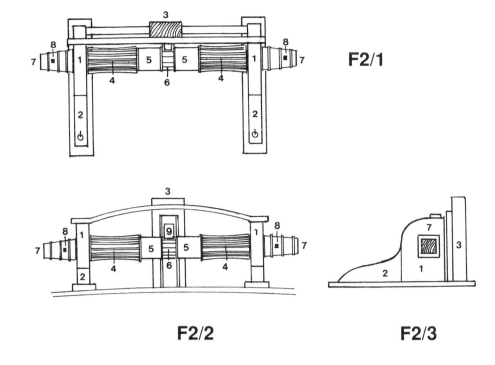

F2/1

F2/2

F2/3

F3 BUCKETS AND THEIR STOWAGE

F3/1 Elevations and plan (1/20 scale)

1. Forward elevation
2. Side elevation
3. Plan
4. Bucket

F3/2 Perspective view (no scale)

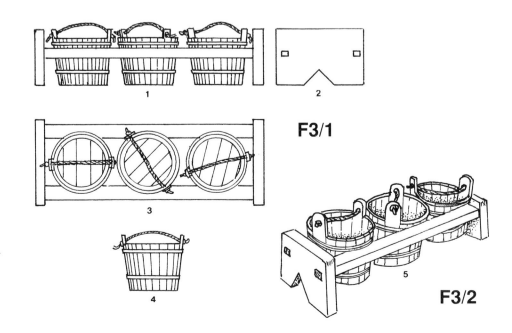

F3/1

F3/2

4   PUMP

4/1   Section (1/50 scale)

.   Handle
.   Rod
.   Leather valve

**4/2   Perspective view of pump handle
(no scale)**

5   FIRE BOX

5/1   Elevations and plan (1/20 scale)

.   Forward elevation
.   Side elevation
.   Plan

5/2   Perspective view (no scale)

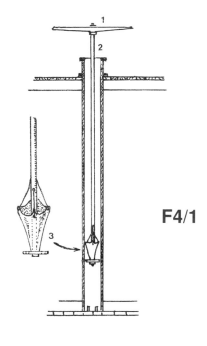

F4/1

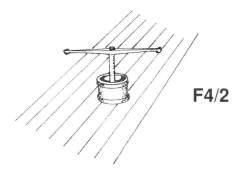

F4/2

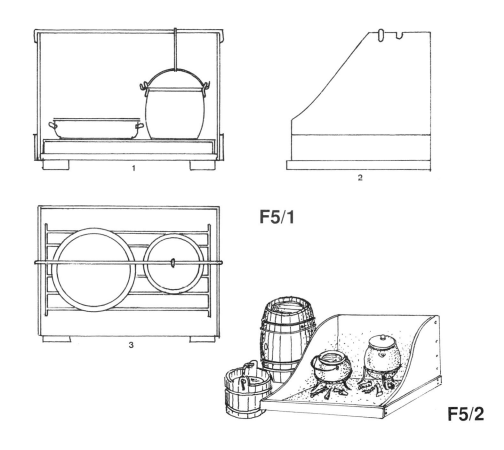

F5/1

F5/2

F Fittings

**F6   BINNACLE (RECONSTRUCTION
        BY GUILLÉN)**

F6/1   Elevations and plan (1/20 scale)

1.   Plan
2.   Front elevation
3.   Side elevation
4.   Light support
5.   Light

F6/2   Perspective view (no scale)

**F6/3   Compass card, from the chart of
         Juan de la Cosa (circa 1500)**

F7   SAND GLASS (no scale)

F6/3

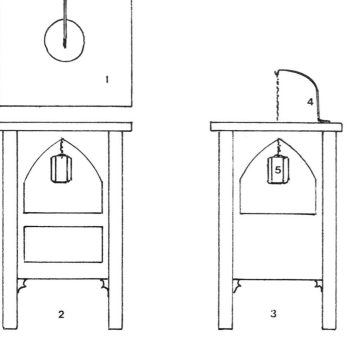

F6/1

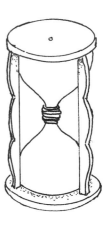

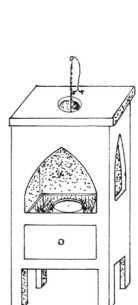

F6/2

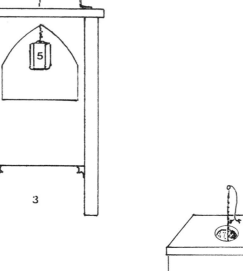

F7

Ground tackle

1 **SHEET ANCHOR (1/50 scale)**

1/1 **Forward elevation**

1/2 **Side elevation**

2 **GRAPNEL (1/50 scale)**

2/1 **Forward elevation**

2/2 **Side elevation**

2/3 **Perspective view (no scale)**

3 **THE REMAINS OF AN ANCHOR FOUND NEAR NAVIDAD FORT (no scale)**

4 **HAWSE HOLE WITH INTERIOR LID (RECONSTRUCTION BY GUILLÉN) (no scale)**

Lid
Wedge
Cross bar

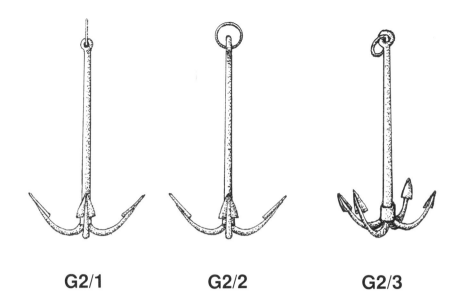

G2/1   **G2/2**   **G2/3**

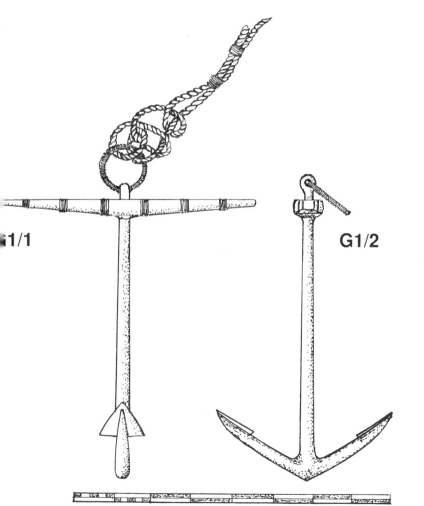

G1/1   **G1/2**

G3

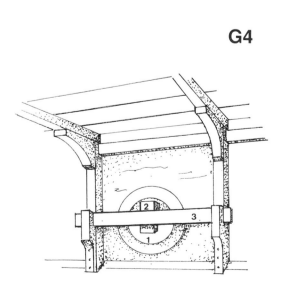

G4

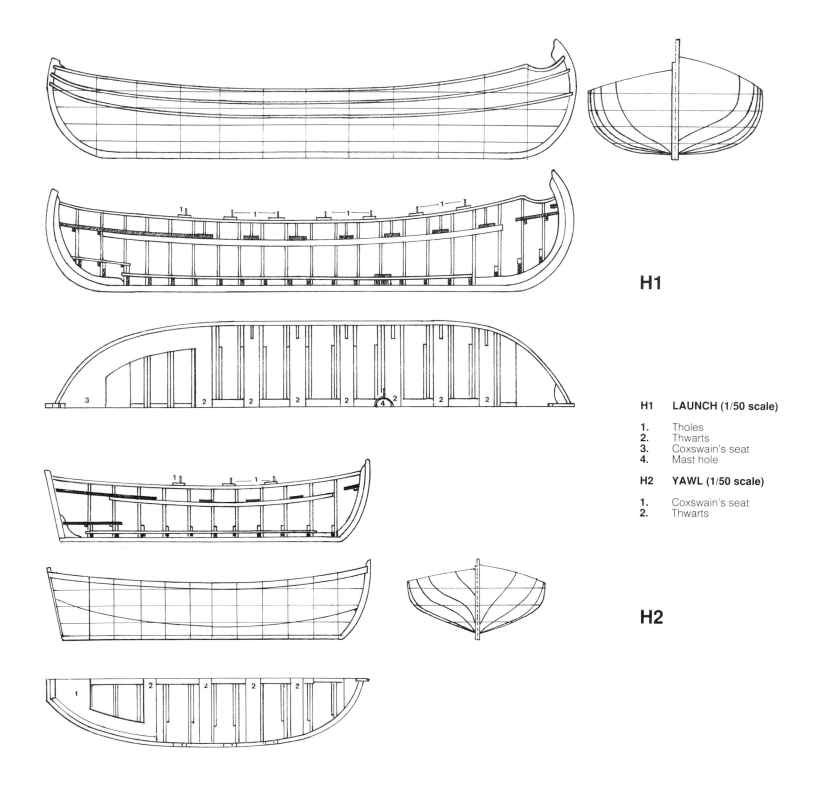

H1

H1 LAUNCH (1/50 scale)

1. Tholes
2. Thwarts
3. Coxswain's seat
4. Mast hole

H2 YAWL (1/50 scale)

1. Coxswain's seat
2. Thwarts

H2

Masts and yards

FOREMAST (1/100 scale)

Forecastle deck
Mast
Truck
Tenon

MAINMAST (1/100 scale)

/1 Forward elevation

Mast
Sheaves
Masthead
Wooldings
Partners
Wedges
Heel
Tenon

/2 Side elevation of masthead

/3 Topsail pole

/4 Perspective view (no scale)

Masthead
Topsail pole
Sheaves

MIZZEN MAST (1/100 scale)

Mast
Truck
Tenon

I1

I2/1

I2/2

I2/3

I2/4

I3

I Masts and yards

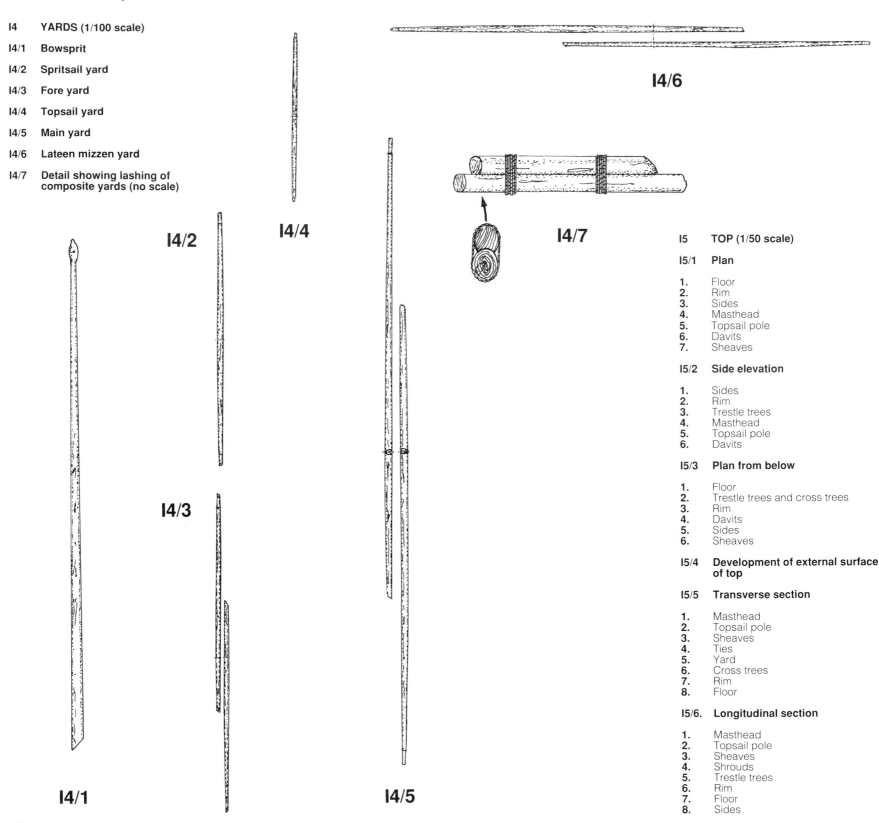

I4   **YARDS (1/100 scale)**

I4/1   **Bowsprit**

I4/2   **Spritsail yard**

I4/3   **Fore yard**

I4/4   **Topsail yard**

I4/5   **Main yard**

I4/6   **Lateen mizzen yard**

I4/7   **Detail showing lashing of composite yards (no scale)**

I4/6

I4/2

I4/4

I4/7

I4/3

I4/1

I4/5

I5   **TOP (1/50 scale)**

I5/1   **Plan**

1.   Floor
2.   Rim
3.   Sides
4.   Masthead
5.   Topsail pole
6.   Davits
7.   Sheaves

I5/2   **Side elevation**

1.   Sides
2.   Rim
3.   Trestle trees
4.   Masthead
5.   Topsail pole
6.   Davits

I5/3   **Plan from below**

1.   Floor
2.   Trestle trees and cross trees
3.   Rim
4.   Davits
5.   Sides
6.   Sheaves

I5/4   **Development of external surface of top**

I5/5   **Transverse section**

1.   Masthead
2.   Topsail pole
3.   Sheaves
4.   Ties
5.   Yard
6.   Cross trees
7.   Rim
8.   Floor

I5/6.   **Longitudinal section**

1.   Masthead
2.   Topsail pole
3.   Sheaves
4.   Shrouds
5.   Trestle trees
6.   Rim
7.   Floor
8.   Sides

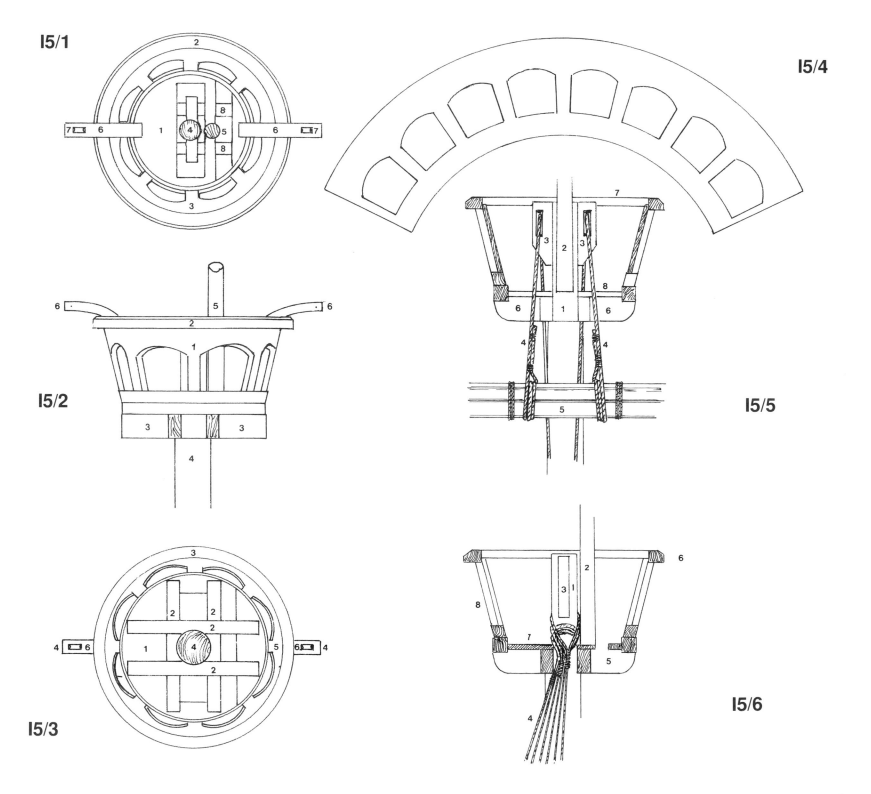

I5/1

I5/2

I5/3

I5/4

I5/5

I5/6

83

J Standing rigging and blocks

J1 GENERAL ARRANGEMENT OF MASTS, STAYS AND SHROUDS
(1/100 scale)

1. Foremast
2. Fore stay
3. Mainmast
4. Main stay
5. Mizzen mast
6. Shrouds
7. Ratlines
8. Tackles

J1

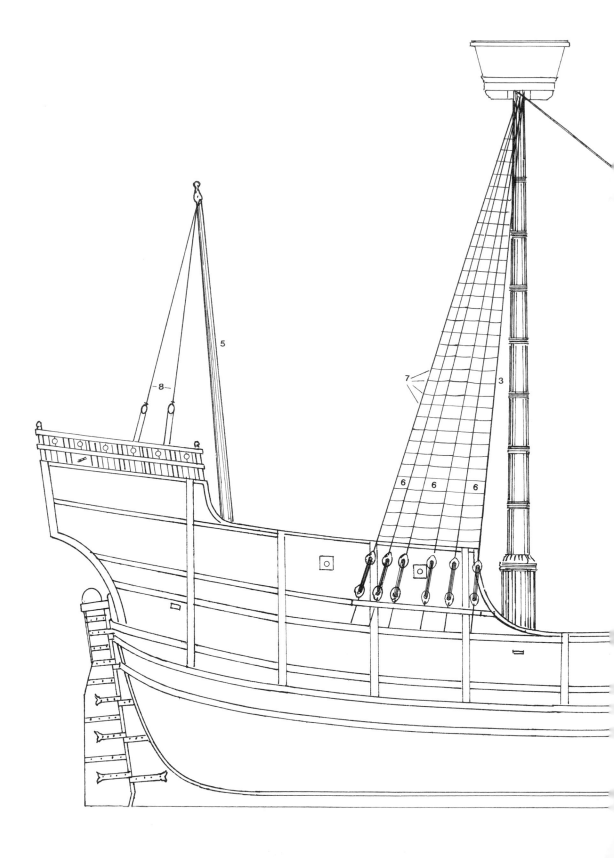

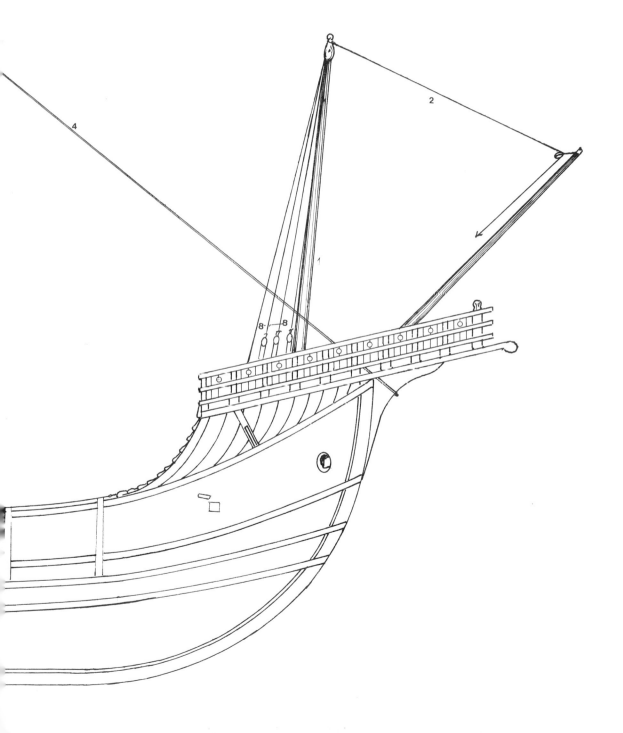

J Standing rigging and blocks

J2 DEADEYES AND BLOCKS (no scale)

1. Double block
2. Upper deadeye
3. Lower deadeye
4. Heart
5. Single block
6. Sheet block

J3 PERSPECTIVE VIEW OF CHANNEL, SHOWING SHROUDS RIGGED WITH LANYARDS AND HEARTS, AFTER FERNÁNDEZ-DURO (no scale)

1. Shrouds
2. Upper and lower hearts
3. Lanyards
4. Channel
5. Chain plates

J4 PERSPECTIVE VIEW OF MAINMAST HEAD (no scale)

1. Sheaves
2. Shrouds
3. Trestle trees and cross trees

J2

J3

J4

J5/1

J5 **RIGGING DETAILS FROM THE MATARÓ MODEL (no scale)**

J5/1 **Blocks**

1. Sheet block
2. Single block
3. Double block
4. Tackle

J5/2 **Perspective view of masthead**

1. Sheave
2. Shrouds
3. Ladder (conjectural)

J5/3 **Parrel**

J5/2

J5/3

K Running rigging to the yards

K1   **PARREL (no scale)**

K1/1   **After elevation**

1.   Mast
2.   Yard
3.   Ribs
4.   Trucks

K1/2   **Method of tightening the parrel (conjectural)**

1.   Parrel ropes
2.   Tackle

K1/3   **Traditional fitting of parrel**

K1/4   **Plan section of mast, yard and parrel**

1.   Ribs
2.   Parrel rope
3.   Trucks

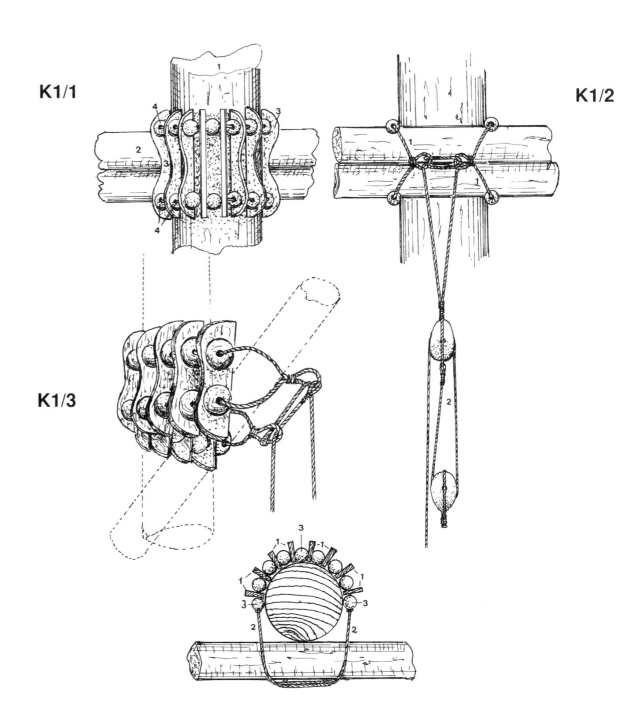

K1/1

K1/2

K1/3

K1/4

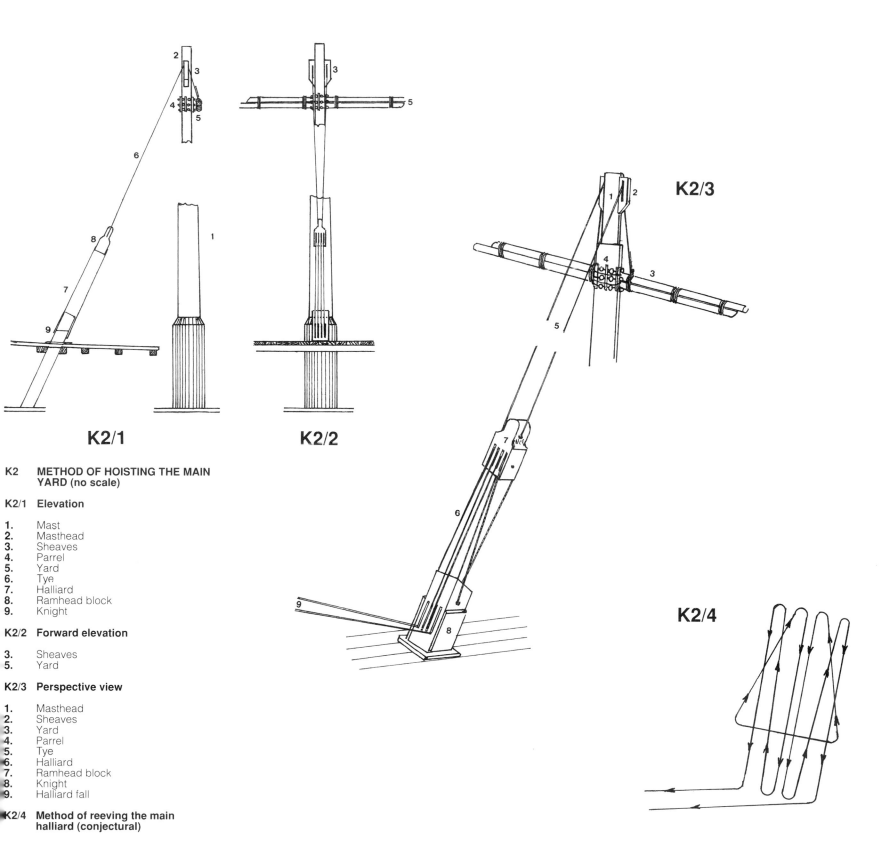

K2/1

K2/2

K2/3

K2/4

**K2   METHOD OF HOISTING THE MAIN
         YARD (no scale)**

K2/1   Elevation

1.   Mast
2.   Masthead
3.   Sheaves
4.   Parrel
5.   Yard
6.   Tye
7.   Halliard
8.   Ramhead block
9.   Knight

K2/2   Forward elevation

3.   Sheaves
5.   Yard

K2/3   Perspective view

1.   Masthead
2.   Sheaves
3.   Yard
4.   Parrel
5.   Tye
6.   Halliard
7.   Ramhead block
8.   Knight
9.   Halliard fall

**K2/4   Method of reeving the main
         halliard (conjectural)**

L Sails

L1 GENERAL ARRANGEMENT OF SAILS (1/150 scale)

1. Spritsail
1. Foresail
3. Topsail
4. Mainsail
5. Bonnet
6. Mizzen sail

L1

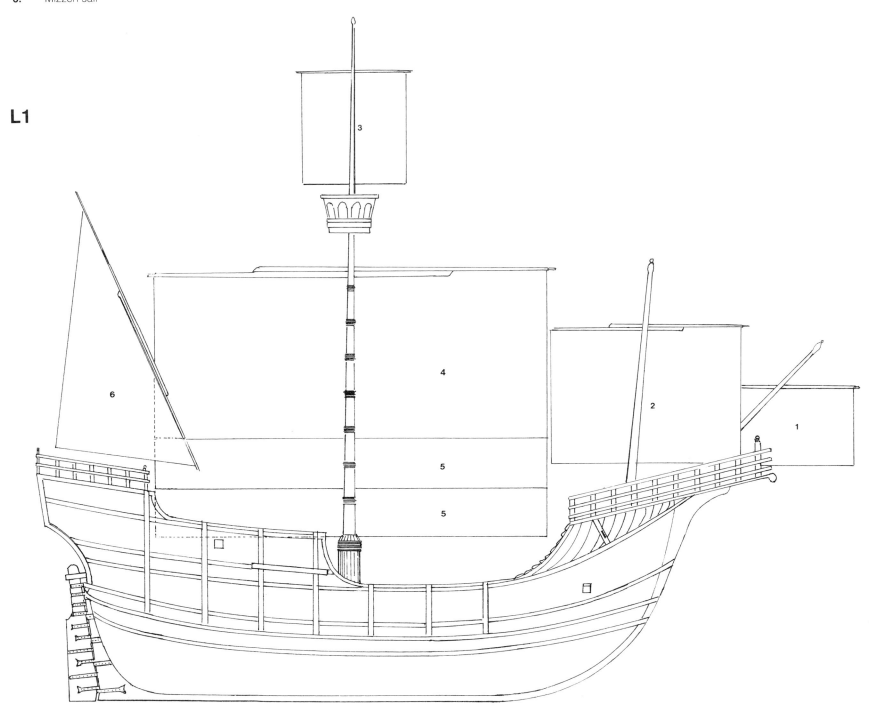

L2 SAILS (1/100 scale)

L2/1 Mainsail and bonnets

1. Mainsail
2. Bonnets

L2/1

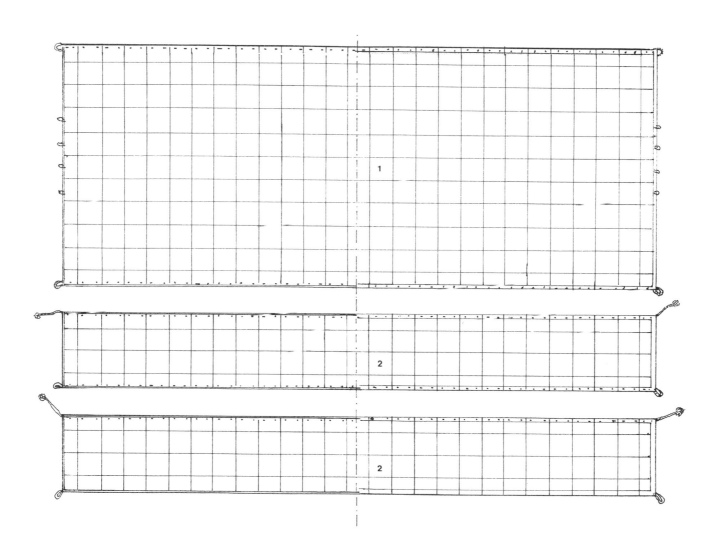

L Sails

L2/2 Other sails

1. Topsail
2. Foresail
3. Spritsail
4. Mizzen sail

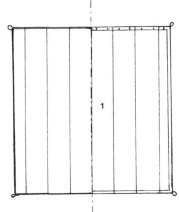

L2/2

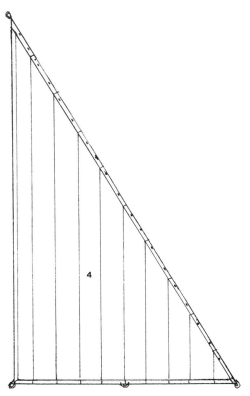

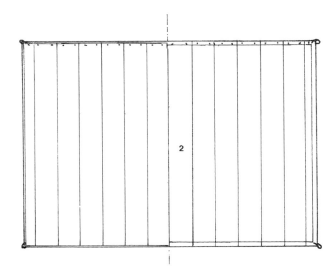

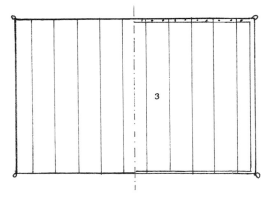

L3 BENDING A SAIL TO A YARD
(no scale)

1. Yard
2. Earring
3. Roband holes
4. Roband
5. Tabling
6. Cringle

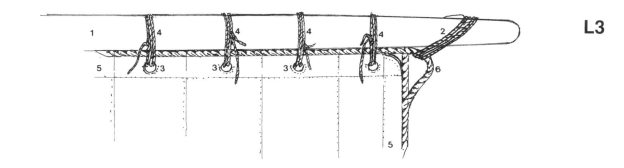

L3

L4 METHOD OF BENDING BONNET
TO SAIL (no scale)

L4/1 Bonnet offered up to sail

1. Mainsail
2. Bonnet
3. Lashing
4. Eyelet

L4/2 Bonnet attached to sail

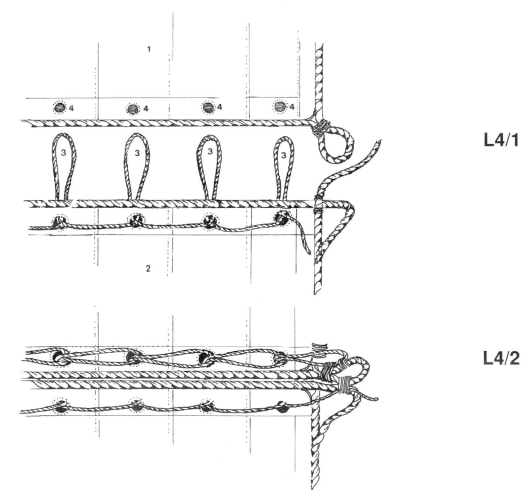

L4/1

L4/2

M1 **SPRITSAIL RIGGING (1/100 scale)**

1. Lifts
2. Braces
3. Sheets

M1

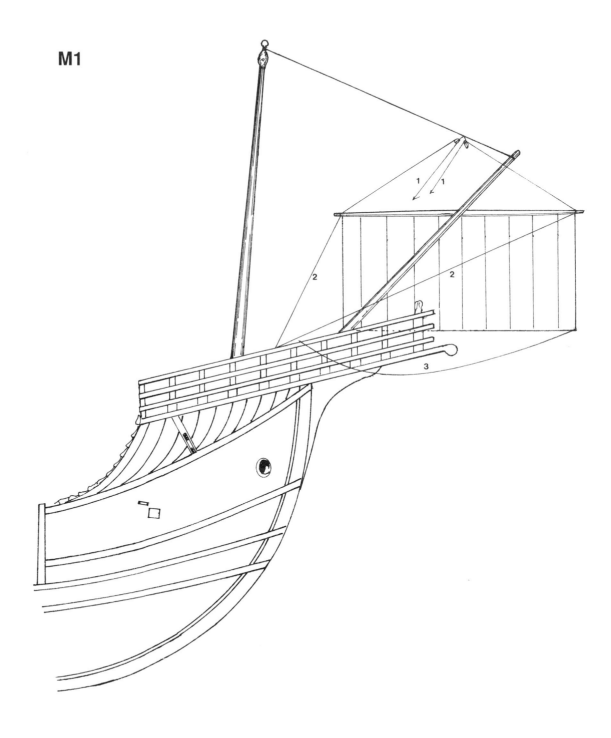

M2 FORESAIL RIGGING (1/100 scale)

1. Lifts
2. Clewlines
3. Brace pendants
4. Braces
5. Bowlines
6. Bridles
7. Tacks
8. Sheets

M2

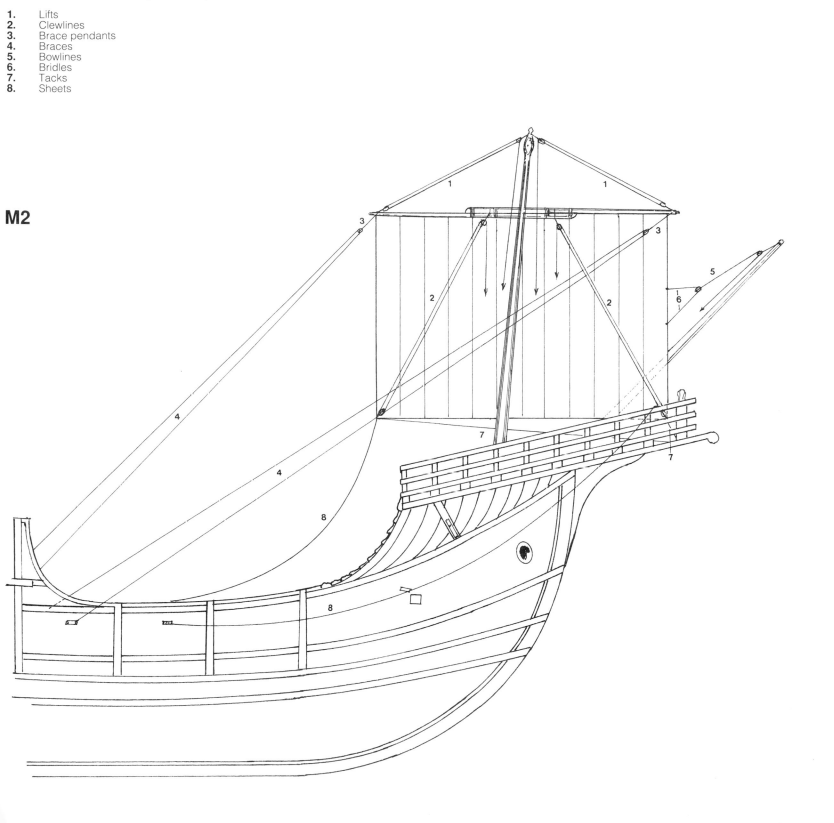

M3 **MAINSAIL RIGGING** (1/100 scale)

1. Lifts
2. Bowlines
3. Bridles
4. Martnet falls
5. Martnets
6. Clewlines
7. Tacks
8. Sheets
9. Brace pendants
10. Braces

M3

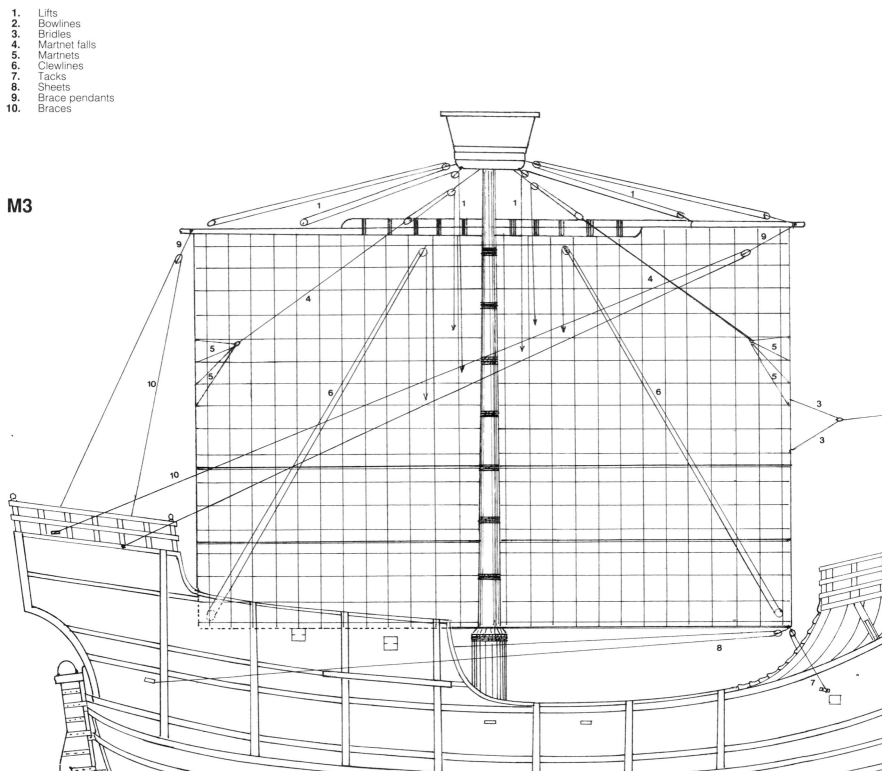

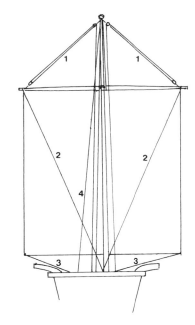

M4 **TOPSAIL RIGGING (1/100 scale)**

1.   Lifts
2.   Braces
3.   Sheets
4.   Halliards

M4

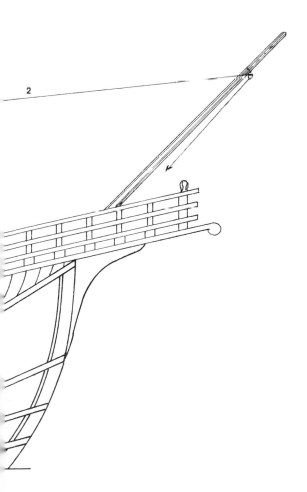

M5 **MIZZEN SAIL RIGGING (1/100 scale)**

1. Cloth
2. Lateen yard
3. *Car*
4. *Pena*
5. *Vangs*
6. Sheets
7. Clewlines
8. Foot brail
9. Tacks
10. *Orsapop*
11. Crowsfeet
12. Yard lift
13. Main top

M5

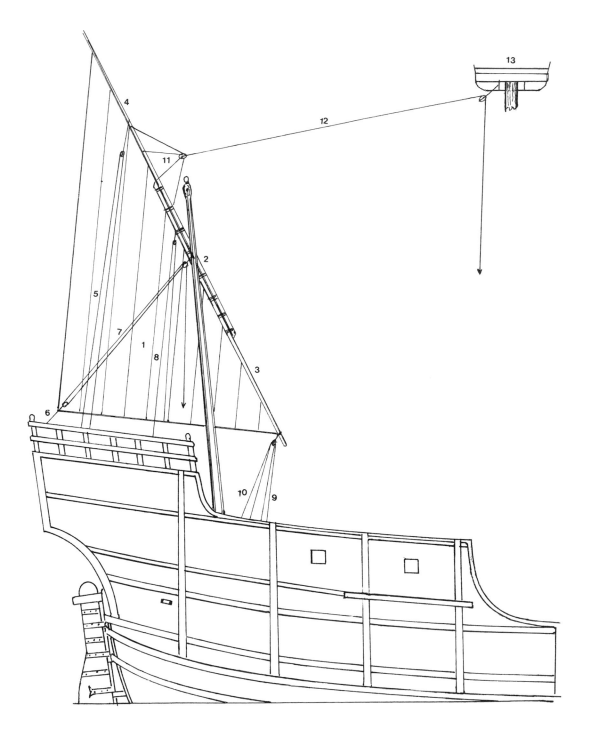

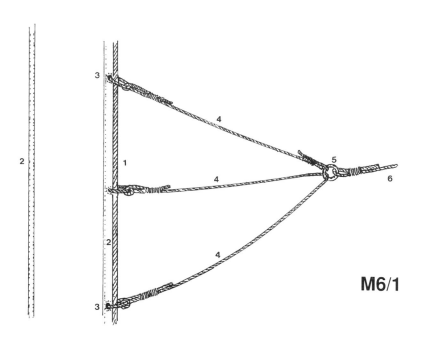

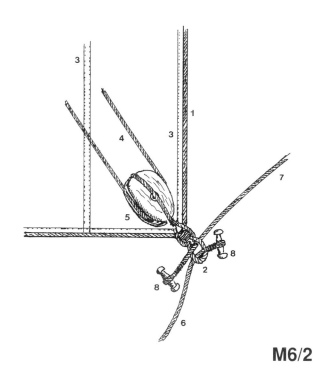

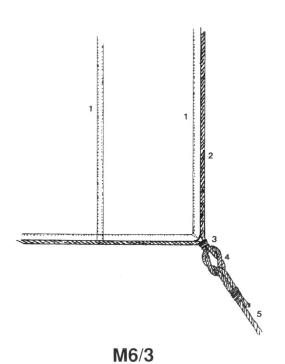

M6 DETAILS OF RIGGING TO SAILS (no scale)

M6/1 Bowline

1. Boltrope
2. Seam
3. Eyelet
4. Bridles
5. Ring
6. Bowline

M6/2 Clew

1. Boltrope
2. Cringle
3. Seams
4. Clewgarnet
5. Block
6. Sheet
7. Tack
8. Toggles

M6/3 Sheet or tack set to the clew with a single knot

1. Seams
2. Boltrope
3. Cringle
4. Sheet bend
5. Sheet

M6/1

M6/2

M6/3

M Running rigging to the sails

M7 DETAILS OF SPRITSAIL RIGGING
(no scale)

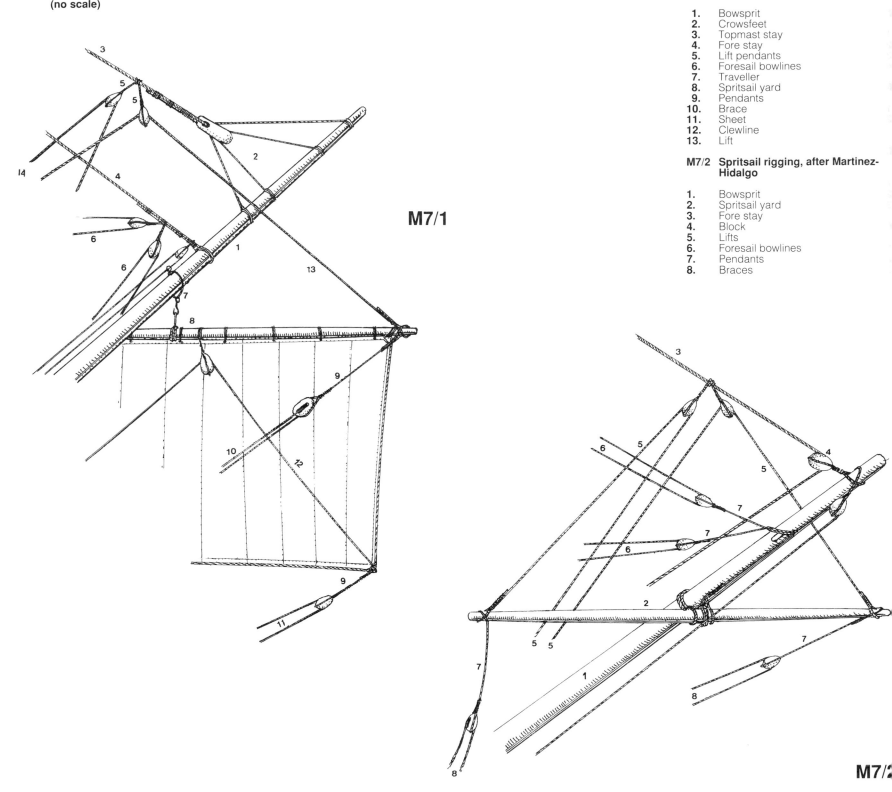

M7/1

M7/2

M7/1 Spritsail rigging, after Guillén

1. Bowsprit
2. Crowsfeet
3. Topmast stay
4. Fore stay
5. Lift pendants
6. Foresail bowlines
7. Traveller
8. Spritsail yard
9. Pendants
10. Brace
11. Sheet
12. Clewline
13. Lift

M7/2 Spritsail rigging, after Martinez-Hidalgo

1. Bowsprit
2. Spritsail yard
3. Fore stay
4. Block
5. Lifts
6. Foresail bowlines
7. Pendants
8. Braces

100

M8 BELAYING POINTS (1/50 scale)

M8/1 Poop rails (port side shown)

1. Main brace sheave
2. Main brace belaying cleat
3. Mooring cleats
4. Block for mizzen tack

M8/2 Forecastle rails (port side shown)

1. Cleats for tackles
2. Cleats for bowlines, braces sheets, traveller, etc

M8/3 Quarterdeck bulwarks (port side shown)

1. Cleats
2. Cleats
3. Gunports

M8/4 Waist bulwarks (port side shown)

1. Sheave for foresail sheet
2. Sheave for foresail brace
3. Cleat
4. Cleat

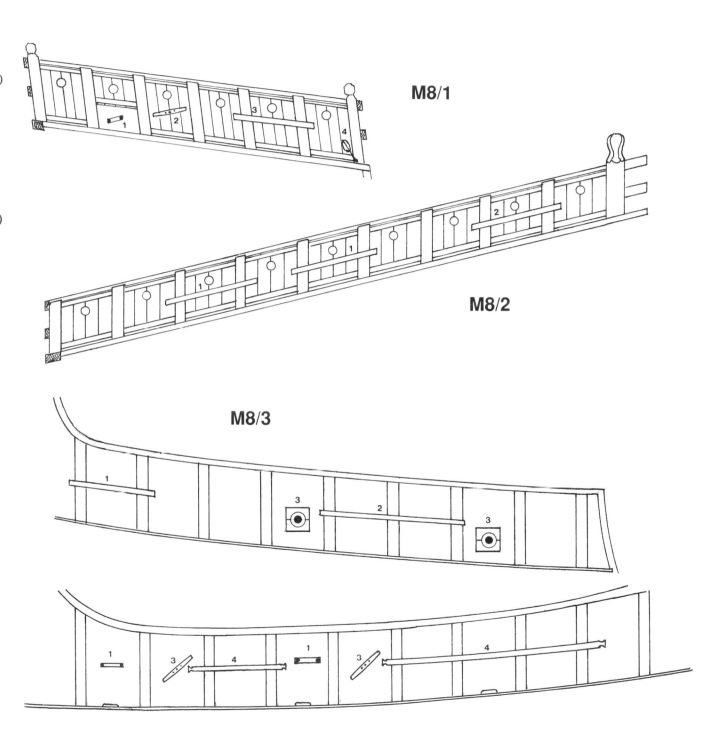

M8/1

M8/2

M8/3

M8/4

N Ordnance

N1/1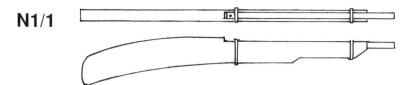

N1/2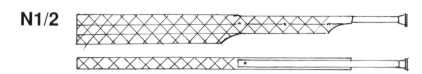

N1/3

N2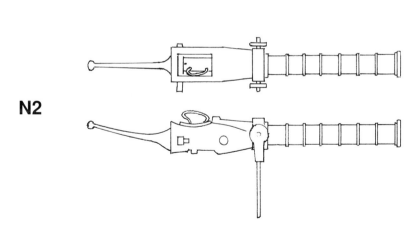

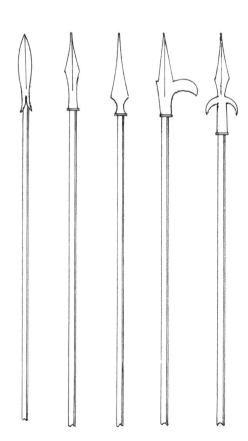

N3

N4   BREECHLOADING LOMBARD
CANNON (1/15 scale)

N4/1   Plan

1. Oak stock
2. Main barrel or hall
3. Chamber
4. Iron wedge
5. Reinforcement rings
6. Suspension rings
7. Trunnions

N4/2   Elevation

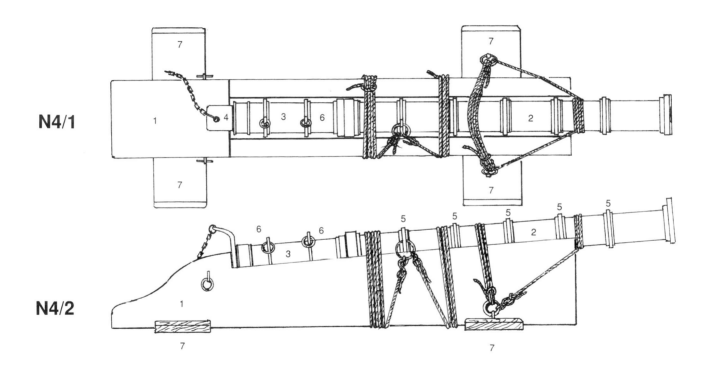

N4/1

N4/2

O Flags

O1 PENNANT (perspective view. About 11m long)

O2 EXPEDITION STANDARD, PRESENTED BY MONARCHS FERDINAND AND ISABELLA OF SPAIN (1/30 scale)

O3 FLAG OF THE KINGDOM OF CASTILLE AND LEON (1/40 scale)

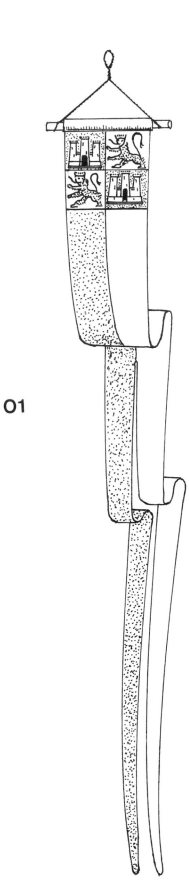

O1

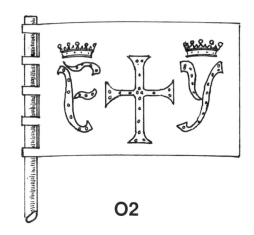

O2

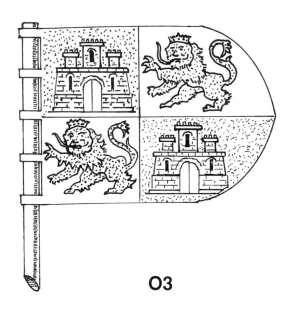

O3

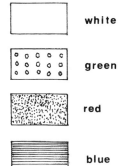

	white
	green
	red
	blue
	purple

04 ADMIRAL'S ENSIGN (1/20 scale)

04/1 Front

04/2 Back

05 ADMIRAL'S ARMS, PRESENTED AFTER THE DISCOVERY OF AMERICA (1/30 scale)

04/1

4/2

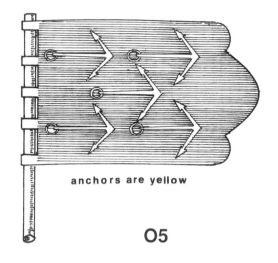

anchors are yellow

O5

P The caravel *Pinta*

P1 GENERAL ARRANGEMENT OF HULL (1/100 scale)

P1/1 Hull profile

1–15. Forward sections
1–18. Aft sections
19. Waterlines
20. Keelson
21. Mast step
22. Floor timbers
23. Futtock rider
24. Deck line

P1/2 Deck plan

1. Forecastle deck (*tilla*)
2. Main deck
3. Quarterdeck
4. Hatchways
5. Mast holes
6. Channels
7. Pin rack

P1/1

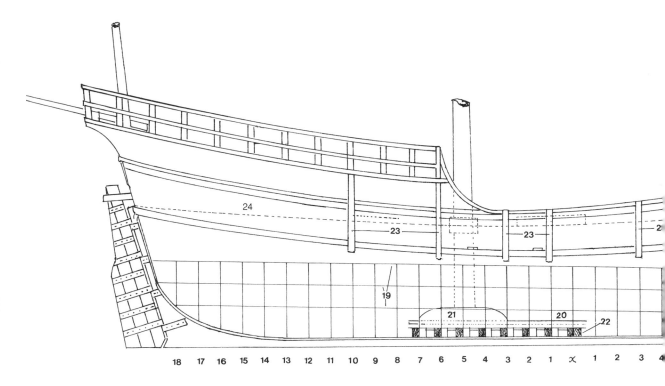

P1/2

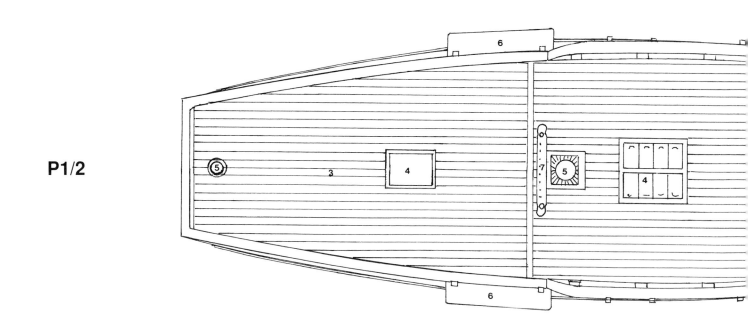

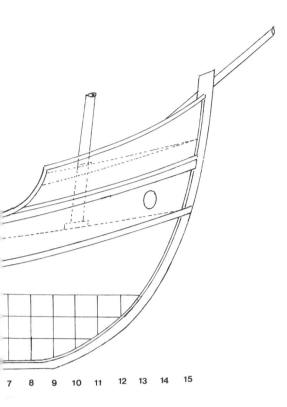

7   8   9   10   11   12   13   14   15

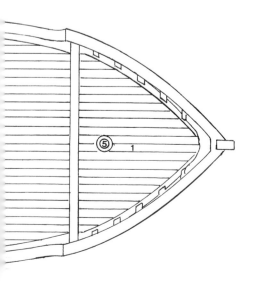

5   1

P The caravel *Pinta*

P2 LINES (scales as marked)

**P2/1 Half breadth plan and station lines
(1/100 scale)**

1–15. Forward sections
1–18. Aft sections
19. Waterlines
20. Diagonals
21. Gunwale line
22. Deck line
23. Hold line

P2/1

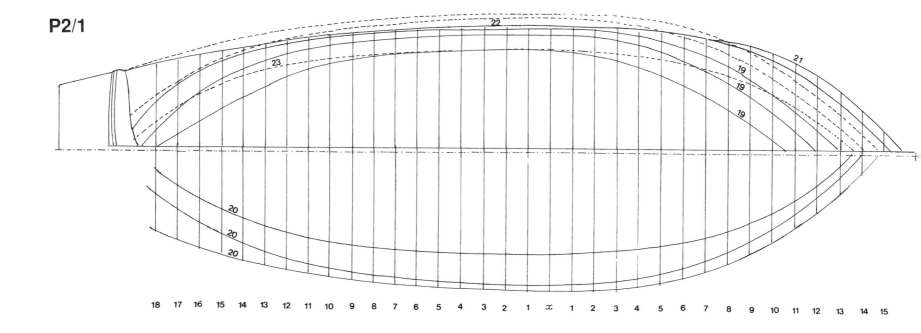

-15. Forward sections
-18. Aft sections
.   Waterlines
.   Diagonals

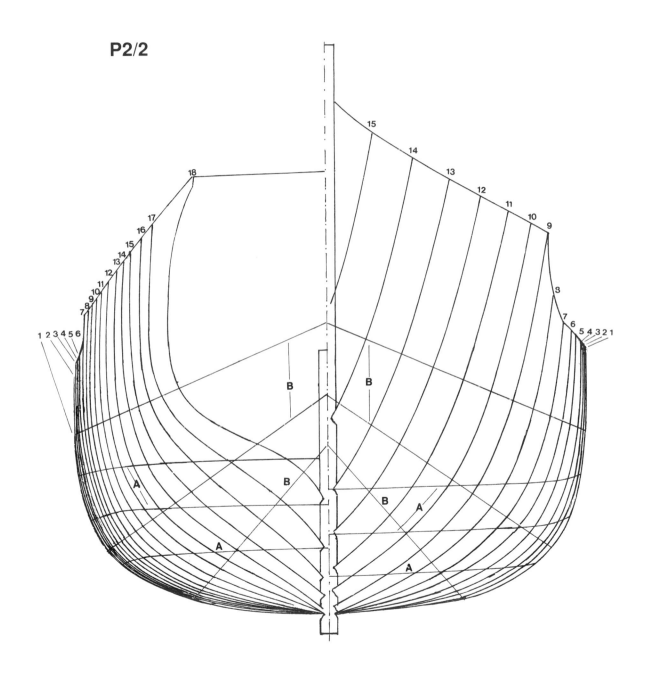

P2/2

P The caravel *Pinta*

**P3 ELEVATION SHOWING MASTING,
RIGGING AND SAILS (1/150 scale)**

1.   Foresail
2.   Mainsail
3.   Bonnet
4.   Mizzen
5.   Fore stay
6.   Lifts
7.   Clew lines
8.   Bowlines
9.   Braces
10. Sheets
11. Tacks
12. Main bowlines
13. Martnets
14. Clewgarnets
15. Mizzen clewline
16. Vang

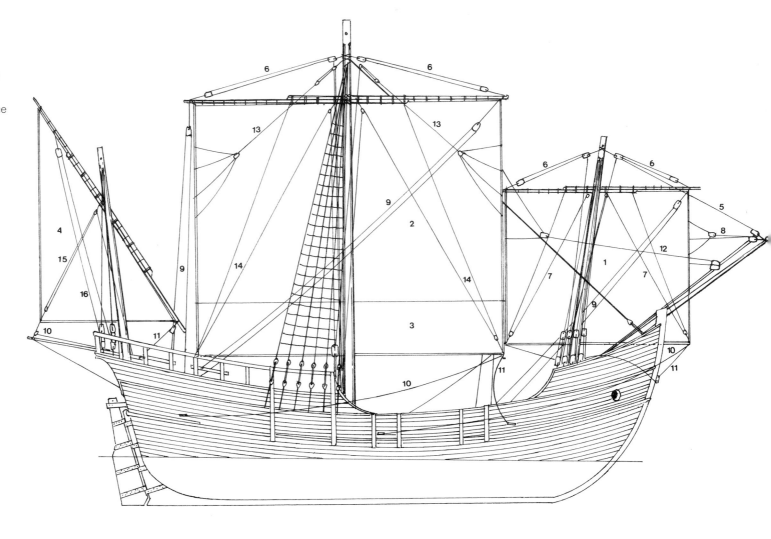

P3

Q The caravel *Niña*

Q1 GENERAL ARRANGEMENT OF HULL (1/100 scale)

Q1/1 Hull profile

1–12. Forward sections
1–17. Aft sections
18. Deck line

Q1/2 Deck plan

1. Forecastle deck (*tilla*)
2. Main deck
3. Quarterdeck
4. Hatchways
5. Masts

Q1/1

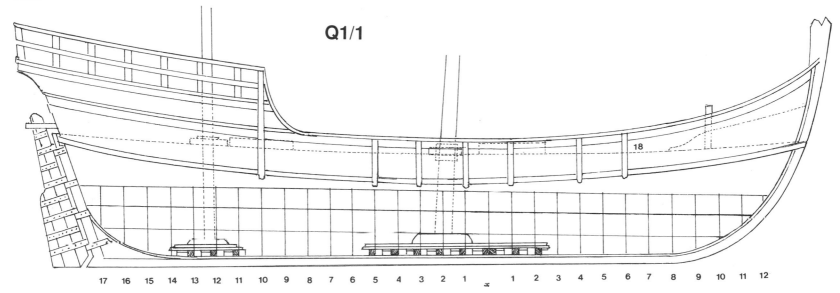

Q1/2

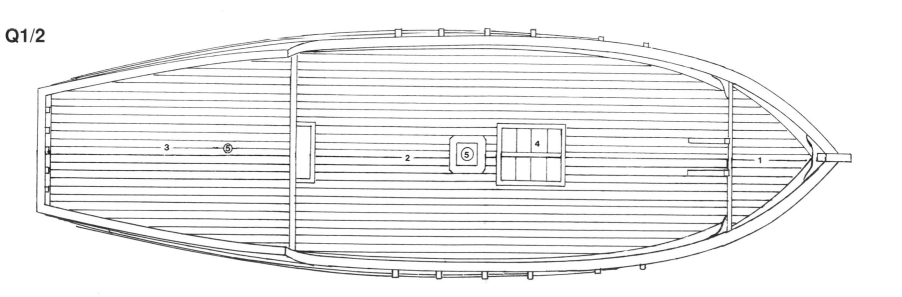

Q2/1

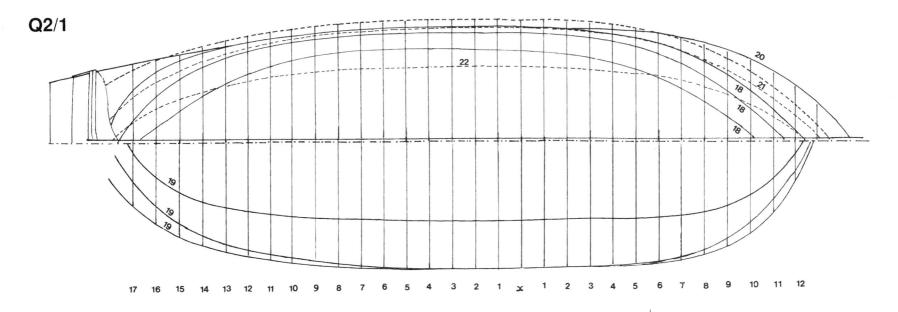

Q2/2

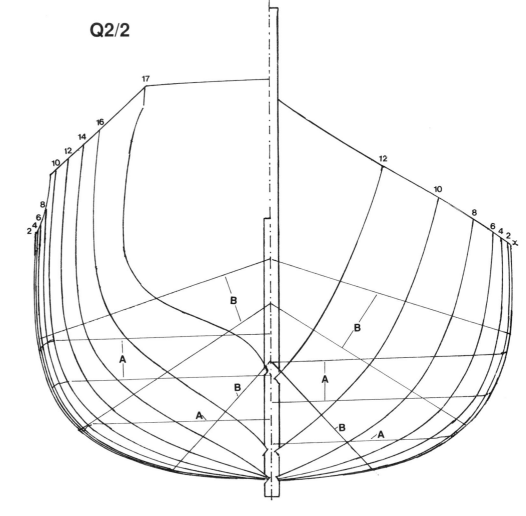

Q2 **LINES (scales as marked)**

Q2/1 **Half breadth plan and station lines (1/100 scale)**

1–12. Forward sections
1–17. Aft sections
18. Waterlines
19. Diagonals
20. Gunwale line
21. Deck line
22. Hold line

Q2/2 **Body plan (1/50 scale)**

X–12. Forward sections
2–17. Aft sections
A. Waterlines
B. Bilge diagonals

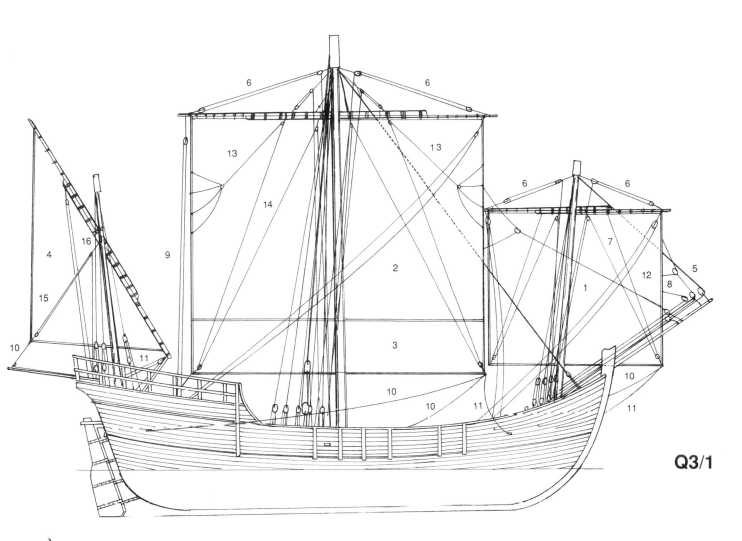

Q3/1

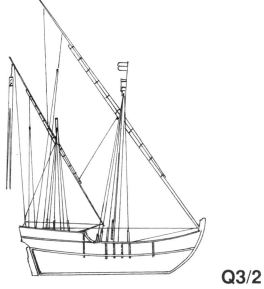

Q3/2

Q3   MASTING, RIGGING AND SAILS
(scales as marked)

Q3/1   Elevation showing masts, sails
and rigging (square rig) (1/150
scale)

1. Foresail
2. Mainsail
3. Bonnet
4. Mizzen
5. Fore stay
6. Lifts
7. Clewlines
8. Bowlines
9. Braces
10. Sheets
11. Tacks
12. Main bowlines
13. Martnets
14. Clewgarnets
15. Mizzen clewline
16. Vang

Q3/2   Elevation showing lateen rig (no
scale)

Q The caravel *Niña*

Q3/3 **Elevation showing *Niña* rigged with four masts, after research by Professor Eugene Lyon (1/150 scale)**

1. Fore sail
2. Mainsail without bonnets
3. Mizzen sail
4. Bonaventure mizzen sail

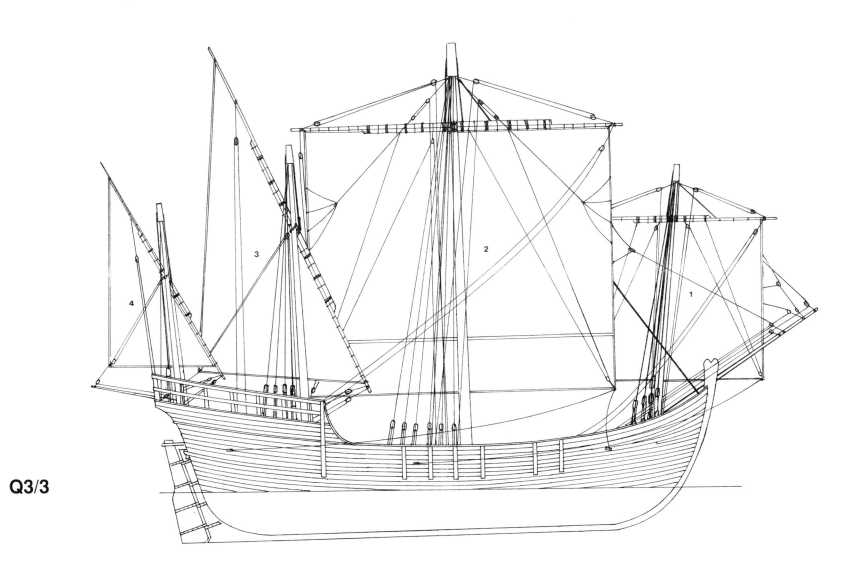

Q3/3

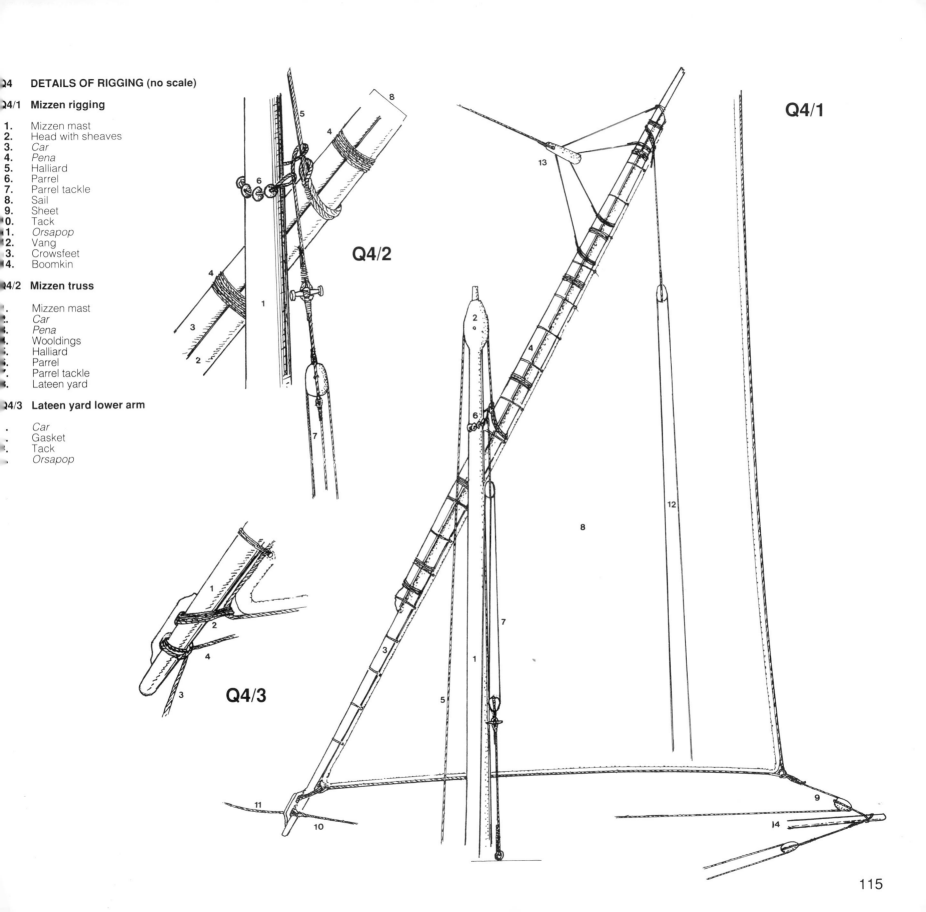

Q4   DETAILS OF RIGGING (no scale)

Q4/1   Mizzen rigging

1. Mizzen mast
2. Head with sheaves
3. *Car*
4. *Pena*
5. Halliard
6. Parrel
7. Parrel tackle
8. Sail
9. Sheet
10. Tack
11. *Orsapop*
12. Vang
13. Crowsfeet
14. Boomkin

Q4/2   Mizzen truss

1. Mizzen mast
2. *Car*
3. *Pena*
4. Wooldings
5. Halliard
6. Parrel
7. Parrel tackle
8. Lateen yard

Q4/3   Lateen yard lower arm

1. *Car*
2. Gasket
3. Tack
4. *Orsapop*

Q4/2

Q4/1

Q4/3

Q The caravel *Niña*

Q4/4 Foresail rigging, seen from forward

1. Yard
2. Halliard
3. Lifts
4. Braces
5. Bowlines
6. Bridles
7. Clewlines
8. Buntline
9. Sheets
10. Tacks

Q4/4

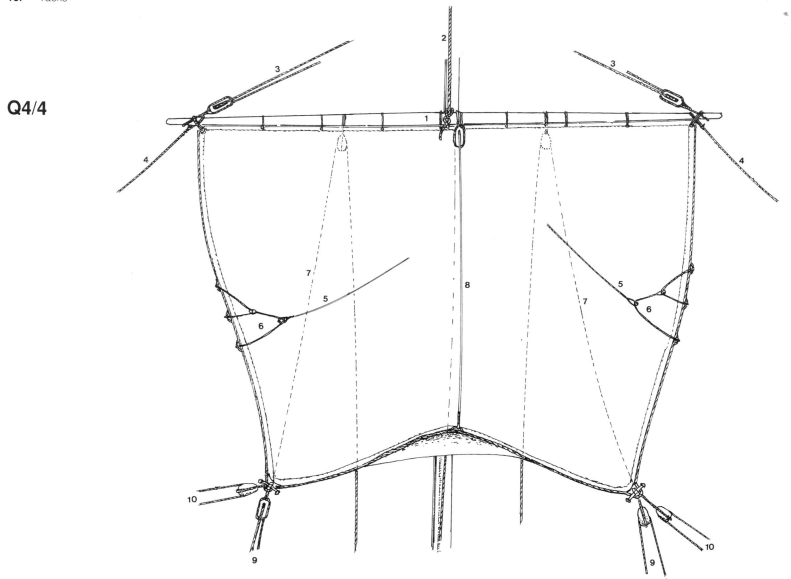

**R1   COMPARISON OF HULLS AND
SAIL PLANS OF FLOTILLA SHIPS**
(no scale)

R1/1   Nao *Santa Maria*

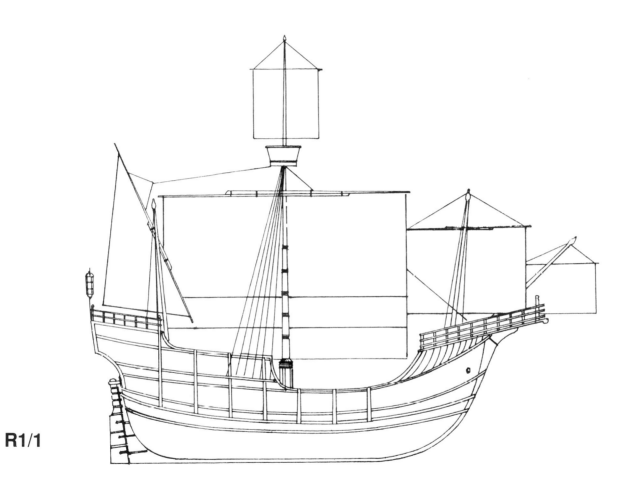

R1/1

R Comparative sail plans

R1/2 Caravel *Pinta*

R1/3 Caravel *Niña*

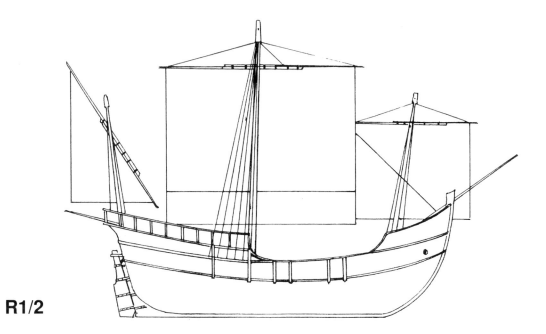

R1/2

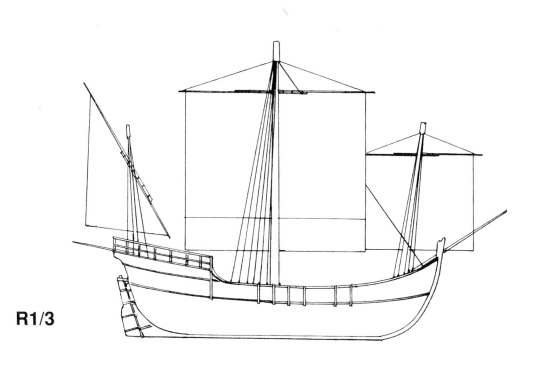

R1/3